Sandy Upp

GW00792521

AS Physical Education
UNIT 2562

OCR

R13161

Module 2562: The Application of Physiological and Psychological Knowledge to Improve Performance

Sue Young and Symond Burrows

Philip Allan Updates
Market Place
Deddington
Oxfordshire
OX15 0SE

tel: 01869 338652
fax: 01869 337590
e-mail: sales@philipallan.co.uk
www.philipallan.co.uk

© Philip Allan Updates 2005

ISBN-13: 978-1-84489-025-5
ISBN-10: 1-84489-025-2

All rights reserved; no part of this publication may be reproduced, stored
in a retrieval system, or transmitted, in any form or by any means, electronic,
mechanical, photocopying, recording or otherwise without either the prior
written permission of Philip Allan Updates or a licence permitting restricted
copying in the United Kingdom issued by the Copyright Licensing Agency Ltd,
90 Tottenham Court Road, London W1T 4LP.

This Guide has been written specifically to support students preparing for
the OCR AS Physical Education Unit 2562 examination. The content has been
neither approved nor endorsed by OCR and remains the sole responsibility of
the authors.

Printed by MPG Books, Bodmin

Environmental information
The paper on which this title is printed is sourced from managed, sustainable
forests.

AS Physical Education

Contents

Introduction

■ ■ ■

Content Guidance

■ ■ ■

Questions and Answers

Introduction

About this guide

This unit guide is written to help you prepare for Unit 2562, which examines the content of **Module 2562: The Application of Physiological and Psychological Knowledge to Improve Performance**. There are three sections to this guide:
- **Introduction** — this provides advice on how to use the unit guide, an explanation of the skills required by Unit 2562 and suggestions for effective revision.
- **Content Guidance** — this summarises the specification content of Module 2562.
- **Questions and Answers** — this provides examples of questions from various topic areas, together with student answers and examiner's comments on how these could have been improved.

An effective way to use this guide is to read through this introduction at the beginning of your course to familiarise yourself with the skills required for AS Physical Education. Try to make a habit of following the study skills and revision advice offered in this section. It may also help to refer back to this information at regular intervals during your course.

The Content Guidance section will be useful when revising a particular topic because it highlights the key points. You may want to tick off topic areas as you learn them to make sure that you have revised everything thoroughly.

The Questions and Answers section will provide useful practice when preparing for the unit test. This practice should increase your awareness of exam-technique issues and maximise your chances of success.

The specification

In order to make a good start to Unit 2562, it is important to have a close look at the specification. If you do not have a copy of this, either ask your teacher for one or download it from the OCR website, **www.ocr.org.uk**.

In addition to describing the content of the module (which sometimes provides detail that could earn you marks), the specification gives information about the unit tests. It is important for you to understand the following key terms used:
- **analysis** — a detailed examination to find the meaning or essential features of a topic
- **characteristic** — a feature or key distinguishing quality
- **definition** — a clear, concise statement of the meaning of a term
- **understanding** — showing clear knowledge of topics covered

The specification also provides information about other skills required in Unit 2562. For example, using the experience gained by performing practical activities as a basis for improving physiological and psychological understanding. You also need to develop the skills of interpreting and drawing graphs and diagrams.

Finally, in addition to looking at the specification, it would be useful for you to read the examiners' reports and mark schemes from previous Unit 2562 tests (these are available from OCR). These documents show you the depth of knowledge that examiners are looking for, as well as pointing out common mistakes and providing advice on how to achieve good grades.

Study skills and revision strategies

All students need good study skills to be successful. This section provides advice and guidance on how to study AS Physical Education, together with some strategies for effective revision.

Organising your notes

PE students often accumulate a large quantity of notes, so it is useful to keep this information in an organised manner. The presentation is important; good notes should always be clear and concise. You could try organising your notes under main headings and subheadings, with key points highlighted using capitals, italics or colour. Numbered lists can be useful, as can the presentation of information in table form and simple diagrams. For example:

It is a good idea to file your notes in specification order, using a consistent series of headings, as illustrated below.

Unit 2562, section B: learning skills in PE
Motivation and arousal
• Definition of motivation
• Knowledge of drive reduction theory (Hull)
• Knowledge of intrinsic and extrinsic methods of motivation

At a convenient time after lessons, it is a good idea to check your understanding of your notes. If anything is still unclear, you could ask a friend to explain, do some further reading, or ask your teacher for help.

Organising your time

It is a good idea to make a revision timetable to ensure you use your time effectively. This should allow enough time to cover all the relevant material. However, it must also be realistic. For many students, revising for longer than an hour at a time becomes counterproductive, so allow time for short relaxation breaks or exercise to refresh the body and mind.

Improving your memory

There are several ways to improve the effectiveness of your memory. Organising the material will help, especially if you use topic headings, numbered lists and diagrams. Reviewing and condensing your notes will also be useful, as will discussing topics with teachers and other students. Using mnemonics (memory aids) can make a big difference. For example, a mnemonic for the key characteristics of skill is:

- **F**luent
- **L**earned
- **A**esthetic
- **G**oal-directed

Revision strategies

To revise a topic effectively, you should work carefully through your notes, using a copy of the specification to make sure everything is covered. Summarise your notes on the key points using the tips offered above. Topic cue cards, with a summary of key facts and visual representations of the material, can be useful. These are easily carried around for quick revision. Finally, use the Content Guidance and Question and Answer sections in this book, discussing any problems or difficulties you have with your teachers or other students.

In many ways, you should prepare for a unit test like an athlete prepares for a major event, such as the Olympic games. An athlete trains every day for weeks or months before the event, practising the required skills in order to achieve the best result on the day. So it is with exam preparation: everything you do should contribute to your chances of success in the unit test.

The following points summarise some of the strategies that you may wish to use to make sure your revision is as effective as possible:

- Use a revision timetable.
- Ideally, spend time revising in a quiet room, sitting upright at a desk or table, with no distractions.
- Test yourself regularly to assess the effectiveness of your revision. Ask yourself: 'Which techniques work best?' 'What are the gaps in my knowledge?' Remember to revise what you *don't* know.
- Practise past paper questions to highlight gaps in your knowledge and understanding and to improve your technique. You will also become more familiar with the terminology used in exam questions.

- Spend time doing 'active revision', such as:
  - discussing topics with fellow students or teachers
  - summarising your notes
  - compiling revision cue cards
  - answering previous test questions and self-checking against mark schemes

Preparation for exams is a very personal thing — you should do what works best for you. You could also draw up, and use, a 'revision progress' table, as shown below.

Revision progress

Complete column 2 to show how far you have progressed with your revision:

- N = not revised yet
- P = partly revised
- F = fully revised

Complete column 3 to show how confident you are with the topic:

- 5 = high degree of confidence
- 1 = minimal confidence — the practice questions were poorly answered

The tables should be updated as your revision progresses.

Section A
Joints, muscles and movement

Topic	Revised (N/P/F)	Self-evaluation (1–5)
Types of joint and their ranges and types of movement (wrist, radio-ulnar, elbow, shoulder, spine, hip, knee, ankle)		
Articulating bones		
Location and action of the muscles surrounding the joint		
Exercises that can improve the strength of these muscles		
Functions of a muscle (agonist, antagonist and fixator)		
Types of contraction (concentric, eccentric and isometric)		
Structure and function of the different fibre types (slow oxidative, fast oxidative glycolytic and fast glycolytic)		
The effect of a warm-up on skeletal muscle tissue in relation to speed and force of contraction		

Mechanics, motion and movement

Topic	Revised (N/P/F)	Self-evaluation (1–5)
Newton's laws of motion		
The types of motion produced		
The effect of size, direction and position of application of force on a body		
Centre of mass		

Make sure you can relate all the above topics to practical examples.

Cardiovascular systems

Topic	Revised (N/P/F)	Self-evaluation (1–5)
The cardiac cycle, the conduction system and the link between them		
Definitions of, and resting values for, heart rate, stroke volume and cardiac output at rest and during exercise		
Neural, hormonal and intrinsic control of the heart		
The distribution of cardiac output (vascular shunt)		
Vasomotor control		
How carbon dioxide and oxygen are carried within the vascular system		
The effects of a warm-up and cool-down period on the vascular system		

Respiration

Topic	Revised (N/P/F)	Self-evaluation (1–5)
The mechanics of breathing (use of the diaphragm and external intercostals)		
Mechanics of breathing during exercise (use of additional muscles — sternocleidomastoid and pectoralis minor for inspiration and internal intercostals and abdominal muscles for expiration)		
Respiratory volumes at rest (definitions and values)		
Changes in lung volumes during exercise (values for sub-maximal and maximal work)		

introduction

Gaseous exchange at the lungs and tissue respiration		
Changes in gaseous exchange at the lungs and in tissue respiration during exercise (increased diffusion gradient and accelerated dissociation of oxyhaemoglobin)		
Neural and chemical control of respiration		
The effect of altitude on the respiratory system		

Section B
Defining, developing and classifying skills

Topic	Revised (N/P/F)	Self-evaluation (1–5)
The characteristics of skilled performance		
Different types of skill		
Analysing movement skills		
The application of 'classification' in the organisation and determination of practices		
Definition and characteristics of abilities		
Development of motor skills		

Information processing

Topic	Revised (N/P/F)	Self-evaluation (1–5)
Basic models of information processing		
Memory process		
Reaction time		
Feedback		

You need to be able to relate the information-processing requirements of movement skills to your own practical activity experiences.

Control of motor skills

Topic	Revised (N/P/F)	Self-evaluation (1–5)
Motor programmes		
Motor control		
Open-loop and closed-loop theories (Adams)		
Schema theory		

Learning skills

Topic	Revised (N/P/F)	Self-evaluation (1–5)
Connectionist or association themes		
Cognitive learning theory		
Observational learning		
Phases of learning movement skills		
Methods of guidance		
Transfer of learning		
Motivation and arousal		
Practice conditions (e.g. massed versus distributed)		

It is important to revise every topic, because any area of the specification could appear in the unit test.

The unit test

The unit test consists of four compulsory structured questions, each worth 15 marks. Each question is broken into parts. The test is divided into two sections:

- Section A — Application of Anatomical and Physiological Knowledge to Improve Performance
- Section B — Acquiring and Performing Movement Skills

Mark allocations vary, but most parts are 2–5 marks. There are 60 marks available in this test, which lasts for $1\frac{1}{2}$ hours (giving you just $1\frac{1}{2}$ minutes per mark).

The questions are short and may use pictures or diagrams as stimulus materials. If reference to the stimulus material is asked for in the question, you must refer to it in your answer. Lines are provided on which to write your answers and additional blank pages are available at the back of the question–answer booklet. You should avoid squashing your answer into the available space because this can make it difficult to read. Do not write answers in the left- or right-hand margin, because these are for the examiner's use. Questions may have some words highlighted. This is to draw your attention to key words or phrases that you need to consider in order to answer the question. Sometimes, questions are followed by 'structured headings'. This is to help you organise your response. Make sure you write the appropriate answer under the correct subheading.

You might be required to sketch or interpret graphs and diagrams. You have to be able to show your understanding of the specification content by using appropriate technical language in your answers.

There are a number of terms commonly used in unit tests. It is important that you understand the meaning of each of these terms and that you answer the question appropriately.

- **Compare** — point out similarities and differences.
- **Define** — give a statement, outlining what is meant by a particular term.
- **Describe** — provide an accurate account of the main points in relation to the task set.
- **Discuss** — describe and evaluate, putting forward the various opinions on a topic.
- **Explain** — give reasons to justify statements and opinions given in your answer.
- **Identify** — show understanding of unique or key characteristics by being able to give something an appropriate 'label'.
- **State/give/list/name** — give a concise, factual answer.
- **What?/why?/where?/who?/how?** — these indicate direct questions, requiring concise answers.

Whatever the question style, you must read the wording very carefully, underline or highlight key words or phrases, think about your response and allocate time according to the number of marks available. Further advice and guidance on answering Unit 2562 questions is provided in the Question and Answer section of this book.

The day of the unit test

On the day of the test, make sure that you have:

- two or more blue/black pens
- a pencil, rubber and ruler
- a watch to check the time
- water in a clear bottle to keep you hydrated
- a calculator

Make sure that you allow plenty of time to arrive, so that you are relaxed.

Read each question very carefully so that your answers are appropriate and relevant. Make sure that your writing is legible (you will not be awarded marks if the examiner cannot read what you have written). If you need more room for your answer, look for space at the bottom of the page or use the spare sheets at the end of the booklet. If you do this, alert the examiner by adding 'continued below', or 'continued on page X'.

Time is sometimes a problem. Make sure you know how long you have for the whole test. If you finish early, check your answers, adding more points to ensure you gain as many marks as possible. This is your one chance to impress the examiner — so take it!

Content
Guidance

Module 2562 comprises two sections. Section A is called **The Application of Physiological and Psychological Knowledge to Improve Performance** and Section B is **Acquiring and Performing Movement Skills**.

Section A helps create a greater understanding of the structure and mechanics of the human body, the function and control of body systems and how they interlink with the physiological make-up of an individual to determine both the standard and effectiveness of performance in a wide range of physical activities.

There are four main topic areas in Section A:
- Joints, muscles and movement
- Mechanics, motion and movement
- The cardiovascular system
- The respiratory system

Section B requires you to develop and show your understanding of effective ways of acquiring and improving movement skills in a variety of physical activities. It requires you to develop theoretical understanding of skill acquisition and to use practical examples to illustrate this understanding.

There are four main topic areas in Section B:
- Defining, developing and classifying skills
- Information processing during skills performance
- Control of motor skills
- Learning skills

You may already be familiar with some of the information in these topic areas. However, it is important that you know and understand this information exactly as described in the specification. This summary of the specification content highlights key points. Therefore, you should find it useful when revising for the Unit 2562 test.

content guidance

Joints, muscles and movement
Joints

- The skeleton is a framework held together by joints.
- Joints are necessary for muscles to lever bones, thus creating movement.
- A joint is formed where two or more bones meet.
- Joints are classified by how much movement they allow.

A **fibrous joint** allows no movement; it is completely fixed. There is no joint cavity and the bones are held together by fibrous, connective tissue. Examples of this type of joint occur in the cranium, facial bones and the pelvic girdle.

A **cartilaginous joint** allows a slight amount of movement. It is called cartilaginous because the bones are separated by cartilage. Examples of this type of joint are where the ribs join the sternum and the vertebrae.

A **synovial joint** allows movement in one or more direction and is the most common type of joint. These joints have a fluid-filled cavity surrounded by an articular capsule. Hyaline/articular cartilage occurs where the bones come into contact with each other. There are six types of synovial joint:

- ball-and-socket joint — hip and shoulder
- hinge joint — ankle, knee and elbow
- pivot joint — radio-ulna and between the axis and atlas in the neck
- saddle joint — thumb
- condyloid joint — wrist
- gliding joint — between vertebrae in the spine

The structure of a synovial joint

Synovial joints have several common features, which are summarised in the table below.

Feature	Structure/location	Function
Hyaline/articular cartilage	Covers the ends of the bones	Prevents friction between the articulating bones
Joint capsule	A tough fibrous layer of tissue encasing the joint	Protects and strengthens the joint
Synovial membrane	The inner layer or lining of the joint capsule	Secretes synovial fluid
Synovial fluid	Fills the joint capsule	Nourishes the articular cartilage; prevents friction
Ligament	Strong, fibrous connective tissue	Provides stability by joining bone to bone
Pads of fat	Fat	Shock absorber
Bursa	A fluid-filled sac located between the tendon and a bone	Reduces friction

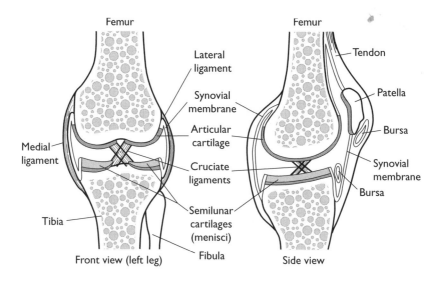

Front view (left leg)   Side view

Movement analysis

Terminology

There are a number of technical terms with which you should be familiar:

- **flexion** — a decrease in the angle that occurs around a joint
- **extension** — an increase in the angle that occurs around a joint
- **abduction** — movement occurring away from the midline of the body
- **adduction** — movement occurring towards the midline of the body
- **rotation** — movement of a bone around its axis, which can be inward (medial) or outward (lateral)
- **circumduction** — the lower end of the bone moves around in a circle, e.g. on rotating the shoulder, circumduction occurs in the bones of the arm
- **lateral flexion** — bending sideways
- **plantar flexion** — bending the foot downwards away from the tibia (standing on your tiptoes)
- **palmar flexion** — bending the hand downwards towards the inside of the forearm
- **dorsiflexion** — bending the foot upwards towards the tibia or bending the hand backwards
- **pronation** — facing the palm of the hand downwards
- **supination** — facing the palm of the hand upwards (carrying a 'soup' bowl may help you to remember!)

Functions of skeletal muscle

A muscle can perform three functions:

- **agonist** — the muscle shortens under tension to produce movement
- **antagonist** — the muscle relaxes or lengthens to allow the agonist to shorten

- **fixator** — the muscle increases in tension, but no movement occurs. A fixator is normally located at the joint where the origin of the agonist occurs. For example, in the upward phase of an arm curl, the bicep brachii contracts and is the agonist. Its origin is on the shoulder, so the deltoid acts as a fixator during this movement.

Synovial joints, movement, muscles and strengthening exercises

These are summarised in the movement analysis tables below.

Ball-and-socket joints

Hip

Articulating bones: acetabulum of the pelvis and femur

Movement	Agonist	Strengthening exercise
Flexion	Ilio psoas	Sit-up
Extension	Gluteus maximus	Bent-knee hip extension
Lateral rotation	Gluteus maximus	
Medial rotation	Gluteus minimus	Side-hip raise
Abduction	Gluteus medius	
Adduction	Adductors (longus, brevis and magnus)	Floor-hip adduction

Shoulder

Articulating bones: glenoid fossa of the scapula and humerus

Movement	Agonist	Strengthening exercise
Flexion	Anterior deltoid	Shoulder press
Extension	Latissimus dorsi	Chin-up
Lateral rotation	Infraspinatus	Bent-over lateral raise
Medial rotation	Subscapularis	
Abduction	Middle deltoid	Back press
Adduction	Pectoralis major	Pec deck
Horizontal flexion	Pectoralis major	
Horizontal extension	Trapezius	Seated row

Hinge joints

Elbow

Articulating bones: radius, ulna and humerus

Movement	Agonist	Strengthening exercise
Flexion	Biceps brachii	Bicep curl
Extension	Triceps brachii	Tricep extension

Knee
Articulating bones: tibia, femur and patella

Movement	Agonist	Strengthening exercise
Flexion	Biceps femoris	Leg curl
Extension	Rectus femoris	Squat

Ankle
Articulating bones: tibia, fibula and talus

Movement	Agonist	Strengthening exercise
Plantarflexion	Gastrocnemius	Toe raise
Dorsiflexion	Tibialis anterior	Heel dip

Pivot joint
Radio-ulna
Articulating bones: radius and ulna

Movement	Agonist	Strengthening exercise
Pronation	Pronator teres	Dumbell curl — downward phase
Supination	Supinator	Dumbell curl — upward phase

Condyloid joints
Wrist
Articulating bones: carpals, radius, ulna

Movement	Agonist	Strengthening exercise
Palmarflexion	Wrist flexors	Wrist curl
Dorsiflexion	Wrist extensors	Reverse wrist curl

Gliding joints
Spine
Articulating bones: vertebral arches

Movement	Agonist	Strengthening exercise
Flexion	Rectus abdominus	Sit-up
Extension	Sacrospinalis	Back extension
Lateral flexion	External obliques	Side bend
Rotation (to the opposite side)	External obliques	Twisting sit-up

Types of muscular contraction

A muscle can contract in three different ways, depending on the muscle action that is required.

Concentric contraction

The muscle shortens under tension. For example, during the upward phase of an arm curl, the biceps brachii performs a concentric contraction as it shortens to produce flexion of the elbow.

Eccentric contraction

The muscle lengthens under tension (and does not relax). When a muscle contracts eccentrically it is acting as a brake to help control the movement of the body part during negative work (e.g. landing from a standing jump). Here, the quadriceps muscles are performing negative work as they are supporting the weight of the body during landing. The knee joint is in the flexed position but the quadriceps muscles are unable to relax as the weight of the body ensures that they lengthen under tension.

Isometric contraction

The muscle contracts without lengthening or shortening. The result is that no movement occurs. An isometric contraction occurs when a muscle acts as a fixator or against a resistance.

Muscle structure

Muscle structure

There are three main types of muscle fibre:
- **type I — slow oxidative** (slow twitch)
- **type IIa — fast oxidative glycolytic** (fast twitch)
- **type IIb — fast glycolytic** (fast twitch)

Skeletal muscles contain a mixture of all three types of fibre, but not in equal proportions. The mix is mainly genetically determined. The fibres are grouped into motor units and only one type of fibre occurs in any one particular unit.

The relative proportion of each type of fibre varies in the same muscles of different people. For example, the leg muscles of an elite endurance athlete will have a greater proportion of slow-twitch fibres and the leg muscles of an elite sprinter will have a greater proportion of fast-twitch fibres. Also, postural muscles tend to have a greater proportion of slow-twitch fibres as they are involved in maintaining body position over a long period of time.

The three types of fibre have specific characteristics that allow them to perform their role successfully. These are summarised in the tables below.

Structural characteristic	Type 1	Type IIa	Type IIb
Size	Small	Medium	Large
Glycogen store	Low	Medium	High
Number of capillaries	Many	Many	Few
Number of mitochondria	Many	Many	Few
Myoglobin concentration	High	High	Few

Functional characteristic	Type I	Type IIa	Type IIb
Contraction speed	Slow	Fast	Fast
Force produced	Low	Medium	High
Aerobic capacity	High	Medium	Low
Anaerobic capacity	Low	High	High
Tendency to fatigue	Low	Medium	High

Physiological effects of a warm-up on skeletal muscle

A warm-up allows for:

- an improvement in the elasticity of the muscle fibres, therefore increasing the strength of contraction
- an increase in the speed of the nerve impulse occurring, which results in a faster speed of contraction
- reduced risk of injury due to an increase in blood flow and oxygen to the muscles
- an increase in the speed and strength of contraction because of:
  - an increase in enzyme activity in those muscles that are warmer
  - the improvement in coordination between antagonistic pairs

What the examiner will expect you to be able to do

When learning the features of a joint, make sure you can relate these to specific joints. For example, the hip and shoulder are both ball-and-socket joints, but their features differ, allowing greater flexibility in the shoulder. Learning the movement analysis tables will provide all the necessary information. Make sure you can apply that knowledge to physical activity. You might be asked to look at a picture of a skill and to analyse the movement at the joints.

Mechanics, motion and movement

Newton's laws of motion

- **Newton's first law of motion** states that every body continues in its state of rest or uniform motion in a straight line, unless compelled to change that state by external forces exerted upon it. For example, a football will remain on the penalty spot unless a force is exerted upon it.

- **Newton's second law of motion** states that the rate of change in momentum of a body (the acceleration for a body of constant mass) is proportional to the applied force and that the change takes place in the direction in which the force acts. For example, the more force applied to a ball, the further and faster it will go.
- **Newton's third law of motion** states that to every action there is an equal and opposite reaction. For example, when jumping up for a rebound in basketball the player pushes down on the ground and there is an equal opposite reaction from the ground as it exerts a force upwards.

Motion

Motion can be:
- **linear** — motion in a straight or curved line as long as all parts move the same distance, in the same direction and at the same speed (e.g. tobogganing in a straight line or the curved flight of a shot put)
- **angular** — movement around a fixed point or axis (e.g. a somersault)
- **general** — movements that are combinations of linear and angular motion (e.g. the javelin throw — on the approach, the body moves in a straight line but during the throwing action, the arm has a circular motion)

Force

A force can be described as a 'push' or a 'pull'. A force can cause a body at rest to move or cause a moving body to stop, slow down, speed up or change direction. It can be measured in terms of:
- the **size** or **magnitude** of the force — this is dependent on the size and number of muscle fibres used
- the **direction** of the force — if a force is applied through the middle of an object, then it will move in the same direction as the force
- the position of **application** of a force:
  - applying a force straight through the centre results in movement in a straight line (linear motion)
  - applying a force off-centre results in spin (angular motion)

Centre of mass

The centre of mass is very simply the point of balance. In the human body, the centre of mass is difficult to define because of its irregular shape. In addition, the body is continually moving, which results in the centre of mass changing. In general, for someone adopting a standing position, the centre of mass is in the hip region.

In order to be in a balanced position, the centre of mass has to be in line with the base of support. If the centre of mass is lowered, stability increases. If the centre of mass starts to move near to the edge of the base of support, over-balancing occurs.

For example, a sprinter in the 'set' position has the centre of mass right at the edge of the area of support. On hearing the starting pistol, the sprinter moves, lifting the hands off the ground and becoming off-balanced. This allows the athlete to fall forward and create the speed required to leave the blocks as quickly as possible.

Other ways to increase stability are by:
- having a wider base, or more bases, of support
- keeping the line of gravity (which extends from the centre of mass vertically down to the ground) within the base of support

What the examiner will expect you to be able to do

The most frequently asked questions on force require knowledge of size, direction and application. Make sure you can give specific sporting examples. Try to ensure that you can relate each of Newton's laws of motion to a practical example.

The cardiovascular system
The structure of the heart

Knowledge of the structure of the heart is assumed and will not be directly examined. However, knowledge of the following will be useful:
- **Blood vessels** — several blood vessels are attached to the heart. They bring either oxygenated or deoxygenated blood to the heart and take it away:
  - The **coronary artery** supplies the heart with oxygenated blood so it can work effectively.
  - The **vena cava** carries deoxygenated blood from the body tissues to the right atrium.
  - The **pulmonary artery** carries deoxygenated blood to the lungs.
  - The **aorta** carries oxygenated blood to the body tissues.
  - The **pulmonary vein** carries oxygenated blood from the lungs into the left atrium.
- **Heart chambers** — the heart is divided into two parts by a muscular wall called the **septum**: each part contains an **atrium** and a **ventricle**. The atria are smaller than the ventricles. They do not require much force because they only have to push blood into the ventricles. The ventricles have thick muscular walls, which contract with great force and push blood out of the heart. The left ventricle is the larger. It pumps oxygenated blood all round the body, whereas the right ventricle only pumps deoxygenated blood to the lungs.

- **Heart valves** — there are four main valves that regulate blood flow, ensuring blood moves in only one direction. They open to allow blood to pass through and then close to prevent back–flow. The **tricuspid valve** is located between the right atrium and right ventricle and the **bicuspid valve** lies between the left atrium and the left ventricle. The **semi-lunar valves** occur at the bases of the pulmonary artery and the aorta, where they leave the right and left ventricles respectively.

The conduction system and the cardiac cycle

The conduction system

When the heart beats, blood flows through it in a controlled manner — in through the atria and out through the ventricles. Heart muscle is described as **myogenic** because the beat starts in the heart muscle itself, with an electrical signal in the **sinoatrial node** (SA node/pacemaker). This electrical signal then spreads through the heart in what is often described as a wave of excitation (analogy has been made to a Mexican wave).

From the SA node, the electrical signal spreads through the walls of the atria, causing them to contract and force blood into the ventricles. The signal then passes through the **atrioventricular node** (AV node) in the atrioventricular septum and down through specialised fibres called the **bundle of His**. This is located in the septum separating the two ventricles. The **bundle of His** branches into two bundle branches and then moves into smaller bundles called **Purkinje fibres** that spread throughout the ventricles. When the impulse passes through these fibres, it causes them to contract.

The cardiac cycle

The cardiac cycle describes the emptying and filling of the heart and involves a number of stages. Systole means contraction; diastole refers to relaxation.

Atrial systole
- Atrial walls contract and blood is forced through the bicuspid and tricuspid valves into the ventricles.
- Ventricle walls relax and the ventricles fill with blood.

Ventricular systole
- Atrial walls relax — blood neither enters nor leaves the atria.
- Ventricle walls contract:
  - Initially, no blood leaves but the pressure of blood in the ventricles increases.
  - Then, the pressure of blood opens the semilunar valves and blood is ejected into the pulmonary artery and the aorta.

Diastole
- Atrial walls relax:
  - Blood enters the atria, but cannot pass into the ventricles because the tricuspid and bicuspid valves are closed.
  - Blood enters the atria and passes into the ventricles as the valves open.

- Ventricle walls relax:
  - Initially, blood neither enters nor leaves the ventricles.
  - Then, blood enters the ventricles from the atria. This is passive ventricular filling
    — it is *not* due to atrial contraction.

Diastole takes 0.5 seconds.

Linking the conduction system with the cardiac cycle

- The link between the conduction system and the cardiac cycle occurs during systole.
- The impulse initiates at the SA node and travels across the atria, causing them to contract.
- The AV node then receives the impulse and conducts it down the bundle of His, the bundle branches and into the Purkinje fibres.
- The ventricles then contract.

Heart rate response to exercise

Cardiac terms

- **Stroke volume** is the amount of blood pumped out by the left ventricle in each contraction. On average, the resting stroke volume is approximately 70 cm^3.
- **Heart rate** is the number of times the heart beats per minute. On average, the resting heart rate is approximately 72 beats per minute.
- **Cardiac output** is the amount of blood pumped out by *each* ventricle per minute. It is equal to stroke volume multiplied by heart rate:

$$\text{cardiac output } (Q) = \text{stroke volume } (SV) \times \text{heart rate } (HR)$$
$$= 70 \times 72 = 5040 \text{ cm}^3 \text{ (5.04 dm}^3)$$

Changes in cardiac output, stroke volume and heart rate during exercise

Regular aerobic training results in hypertrophy of the cardiac muscle, i.e. the heart gets bigger. This affects stroke volume and heart rate, and therefore cardiac output. A bigger heart pumps out more blood per beat (increased stroke volume). In other words, the end diastolic volume of the ventricle increases. If the ventricle can contract with more force and push out more blood, the heart does not have to beat so often. Therefore, the resting heart rate decreases. This is called **bradycardia**. The increase in stroke volume and decrease in resting heart rate mean that cardiac output at rest remains unchanged. However, during exercise, an increase in heart rate, coupled with the increase in stroke volume, results in an increase in cardiac output.

The following table shows the differences in cardiac output (to the nearest litre, i.e. dm^3) in a trained and an untrained individual at rest and during exercise. The individuals are aged 18, so their maximum heart rate is 202 beats per minute (bpm). (Maximum heart rate is calculated as 220 minus a person's age.)

Individual	Condition	SV/cm³	HR/bpm	Q/dm³
Untrained	Rest	70	72	5
	Exercise	120	202	24
Trained	Rest	85	60	5
	Exercise	170	202	34

This increase in cardiac output has huge benefits for trained individuals. It means that more blood, and therefore more oxygen, is transported to the working muscles. In addition, when the body starts to exercise, the distribution of blood flow changes — a higher proportion of blood passes to the working muscles and less goes to other organs.

Varying intensities of workload and recovery

The heart rate response to maximal and sub-maximal exercise and during recovery from exercise is shown on the graphs below.

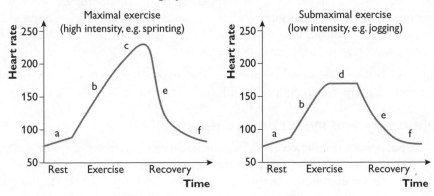

Key to the graphs:

a = anticipatory rise due to the action of the hormone adrenaline

b = sharp rise in heart rate, mainly due to anaerobic work

c = heart rate continuing to rise due to maximal workloads stressing the anaerobic systems

d = steady state as the athlete is able to meet the oxygen demand

e = rapid decline in heart rate as soon as the exercise stops

f = slower recovery as body systems return to resting levels

Control of blood supply

Control of heart rate

Neural control

This involves the **autonomic nervous system**:

- The **sympathetic system** stimulates the heart to beat faster via the cardiac accelerator nerve.

- The **parasympathetic system** returns the heart to its resting level via the vagus nerve.

These two systems are coordinated by the **cardiac control centre** located in the medulla oblongata of the brain. The cardiac control centre is stimulated by:
- **chemoreceptors** (which detect chemical changes)
- **baroreceptors** (which detect a change in blood pressure)
- **proprioceptors** (which detect movement)

This centre then sends an impulse through either the sympathetic or parasympathetic systems to the sinoatrial node of the heart.

Hormonal control
Adrenaline and **noradrenaline** stimulate the SA node (pacemaker) and increase both the speed *and* force of muscle contraction.

Intrinsic control
During exercise, the heart becomes warmer, so heart rate increases. (A drop in temperature results in a reduced heart rate.) In addition, venous return (see page 27) increases, which stretches the cardiac muscle, stimulating the SA node. This, in turn, increases heart rate and the force of contraction. As a result, stroke volume increases.

Starling's law states that stroke volume is dependent on venous return, i.e. an increase in venous return results in an increase in stroke volume.

Pulmonary and systemic circulations
- The **pulmonary circulation** sends deoxygenated blood from the heart to the lungs and returns oxygenated blood from the lungs to the heart.
- The **systemic circulation** sends oxygenated blood from the heart to the body tissues and returns deoxygenated blood from the body tissues to the heart.

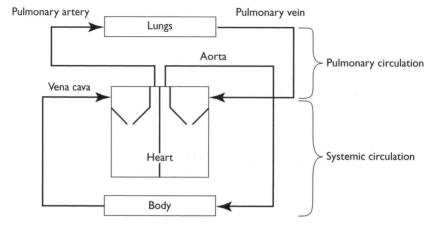

Blood vessels
The types and structure of blood vessels are not directly examined. However, knowledge of the following will be a great help to candidates.

The vascular system consists of five different types of blood vessel that carry the blood from the heart, distribute it round the body and return it to the heart. The order in which the blood flows through the vascular system is as follows:

heart $\rightarrow$ arteries $\rightarrow$ arterioles $\rightarrow$ capillaries $\rightarrow$ venules $\rightarrow$ veins $\rightarrow$ heart

Important features of arteries, capillaries and veins are summarised in the table below.

Feature	Artery	Capillary	Vein
Tunica externa — outer layer containing collagen fibres	Present	Absent	Present
Tunica media — middle layer made up of elastic fibres and smooth muscle	Thick with many elastic fibres	Absent	Thinner than in an artery
Tunica interna — inner layer made up of thin epithelial cells that are smooth to reduce friction	Present	Present	Present
Size of lumen	Small	Microscopic	Large
Valves	Absent	Absent	Present

Venous return

This is the term used for blood that is returned to the right-hand side of the heart through the veins.

At rest, 70% of the total blood volume is contained in the veins. This provides a large reservoir of blood that can be returned rapidly to the heart when needed. The heart can only pump out as much blood as it receives, so cardiac output is dependent on venous return. A rapid increase in venous return enables a significant increase in stroke volume and, therefore, cardiac output. Veins have a large lumen and offer little resistance to blood flow. By the time that blood enters the veins, blood pressure is low. This means that active mechanisms are needed to ensure venous return:

- **Skeletal muscle pump** — when muscles contract and relax they change shape. This change in shape means that the muscles press on nearby veins, causing a pumping effect and squeezing the blood towards the heart.
- **Respiratory pump** — when muscles contract and relax during inspiration and expiration, pressure changes occur in the thoracic and abdominal cavities. These pressure changes compress the nearby veins and enable blood to return to the heart.
- **Valves** — it is important that blood in the veins flows in only one direction. The presence of valves ensures that this happens. This is because once the blood has passed through a valve, the valve closes, preventing the blood from flowing back.

In addition, **gravity** assists the flow of blood from body parts above the heart.

Vasomotor control

The **vasomotor centre** in the medulla of the brain controls blood pressure and blood flow. The vasomotor centre is stimulated by:

- chemoreceptors, which detect chemical change
- baroreceptors, which respond to changes in blood pressure

Blood flow is then redistributed through **vasodilation** and **vasoconstriction**. Vasodilation increases blood flow; vasoconstriction decreases blood flow.

The vascular shunt

During exercise, the working muscles need more oxygen. Vasodilation of the vessels supplying muscles occurs, which increases blood flow and brings in much-needed oxygen. At the same time, vasoconstriction occurs in the arterioles supplying non-essential organs. This redirection of blood flow is called the vascular shunt.

Pre-capillary sphincters also aid blood redistribution. These are tiny rings of muscle located at the openings of capillaries. When they contract, the blood flow through the capillaries is restricted; when they relax, blood flow is increased. During exercise, the capillary networks supplying skeletal muscle have relaxed pre-capillary sphincters. Therefore, the blood flow to the muscles is increased and the tissues are saturated with oxygen.

Transport of oxygen and carbon dioxide in the vascular system

During exercise, when oxygen diffuses into the capillaries in the lungs, 3% dissolves in plasma and 97% combines with haemoglobin in red blood cells, forming oxyhaemo-globin. At the tissues, oxyhaemoglobin dissociates, releasing oxygen. This happens because of the lower partial pressure of oxygen in the muscles. In the muscle, oxygen is picked up by myoglobin. This has a high affinity for oxygen and acts as an oxygen store. Numerous mitochondria within the skeletal muscles use the oxygen for aerobic respiration, producing the energy needed for muscular contraction.

Carbon dioxide is transported in one of three ways:
- 7% dissolves in plasma
- 23% combines with haemoglobin to form carbaminohaemoglobin
- 70% combines with water as hydrogencarbonate ions (carbonic acid)

The effects of warm-up and cool-down periods on the vascular system

Warm-up

A warm-up period helps to prepare the body for exercise:
- The vasomotor centre ensures that vasodilation occurs, so that more blood flows (due to the increase in cardiac output) to the working muscles. This increases the amount of oxygen being transported to the working muscles.
- The warm-up allows for an increase in body and muscle temperatures. This results

in an increase in the rate of transport of the enzymes necessary for the energy systems and muscle contraction.
- An increase in muscle and body temperatures decreases blood viscosity. This improves blood flow to the working muscles. In addition, an increase in temperature results in oxygen dissociating from oxyhaemoglobin more quickly.
- A warm-up delays the onset of blood lactic acid (OBLA).

Cool-down

Any activity (such as a gentle jog) that keeps the heart rate elevated, allows the body to take in extra oxygen. This can reduce recovery time.
- An active cool-down keeps the respiratory and skeletal muscle pumps working. This prevents blood pooling in the veins and maintains venous return.
- The capillaries stay dilated and the muscles are flushed with oxygenated blood. This increases the removal of lactic acid and carbon dioxide.

What the examiner will expect you to be able to do

- Remember that:
  - pulmonary circulation is heart ⟶ lungs ⟶ heart
  - systemic circulation is heart ⟶ body ⟶ heart
- You are expected to be able to relate the conduction system to the cardiac cycle, so do not learn them as two separate systems.
- Always label and explain graphs, in case what you have drawn is not clear to the examiner.
- In questions on neural control of the heart, you might have to relate this to an increase in carbon dioxide.

The respiratory system
The structure of the lungs

Knowledge of lung structure is assumed and will not be examined directly. Some important points are given below:
- The lungs occur in the thorax and are protected by the rib cage.
- The right lung is slightly larger than the left. It has three lobes (sections), whereas the left lung has two lobes.
- The lungs are surrounded by the pleura, which is a double layer of membrane that contains lubricating pleural fluid to reduce friction.
- The lungs are separated from the abdomen by the diaphragm, which is a large sheet of skeletal muscle.

Air, containing oxygen, travels from the atmosphere, passing through several structures before it reaches the bloodstream. The order in which it travels is as follows:

nose $\rightarrow$ pharynx $\rightarrow$ trachea $\rightarrow$ bronchus (right or left) $\rightarrow$ bronchioles $\rightarrow$ alveoli

The alveoli are where the exchange of gases between the lungs and the blood takes place. Their structure is designed to help gaseous exchange:
- Their walls are very thin — only one cell thick.
- They have a dense capillary network.
- They have a huge total surface area to allow maximal oxygen uptake.

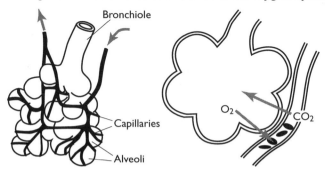

The mechanics of breathing

Air moves from an area of high pressure to an area of low pressure. The greater the difference in pressure, the faster air will flow. Changing the volume of the thoracic cavity alters the pressure of air in the lungs. Increasing the volume decreases the pressure, drawing air into the lungs from outside. Reducing the volume increases the pressure and air is forced out of the lungs.
- Inspiration — the volume of the thoracic cavity increases because of muscular contraction
- Expiration — the volume of the thoracic cavity is reduced

Respiratory muscles

Ventilation phase	Muscles used during breathing at rest	Muscles used during exercise
Inspiration	Diaphragm External intercostals	Diaphragm External intercostals Sternocleidomastoid Pectoralis minor
Expiration	Diaphragm and external intercostals relax (passive process)	Internal intercostals Abdominals

Note that during exercise, additional muscles are used during inspiration and that expiration is active, rather than passive.

Definitions and values of respiratory volumes

Definitions and values of respiratory volumes, together with the way they change during exercise, are given in the table below.

Lung volume or capacity	Definition	Average value at rest/litres	Average value during exercise/litres	Change during exercise
Tidal volume	Volume of air breathed in or out per breath	0.5	2.8	Increase
Inspiratory reserve volume	Volume of air that can be forcibly inspired after a normal breath	3.1	2.0	Decrease
Expiratory reserve volume	Volume of air that can be forcibly expired after a normal breath	1.2	1.0	Slight decrease
Residual volume	Volume of air that remains in the lungs after maximum expiration	1.2	1.2	Remains the same
Vital capacity	Volume of air forcibly expired after maximum inspiration in one breath	4.8	4.8	Remains the same
Minute ventilation	Volume of air breathed in or out per minute	6–7.5/min	120–180/min	Increases
Total lung capacity	Vital capacity + residual volume	6.0	6.0	Remains the same

Gaseous exchange in the lungs

The idea of **partial pressure** is often used when describing gaseous exchange. All gases exert a pressure. Oxygen makes up approximately 21% of air, so it exerts a partial pressure. Gases flow from an area of high pressure to an area of low pressure. As oxygen moves from the alveoli to the blood and then to the muscle, its partial pressure in each has to be successively lower.

The partial pressure of oxygen in the alveoli is higher than the partial pressure of oxygen in the blood vessels, so oxygen diffuses into the blood. During exercise, the working muscles use oxygen so the concentration of oxygen in the muscle is lowered and therefore so is its partial pressure. Oxygen diffuses from the blood and combines with myoglobin in the muscle cells

The difference between any two pressures is referred to as the pressure gradient, and the bigger this gradient, the faster diffusion will be. Oxygen diffuses from the alveoli into the blood, then from the blood to the muscle cells until the pressure is equal.

The movement of carbon dioxide occurs similarly, but in reverse order — from the muscle cells to the blood to the alveoli.

Haemoglobin saturation

The relationship between oxygen and haemoglobin can be represented by the oxyhaemoglobin dissociation curve:

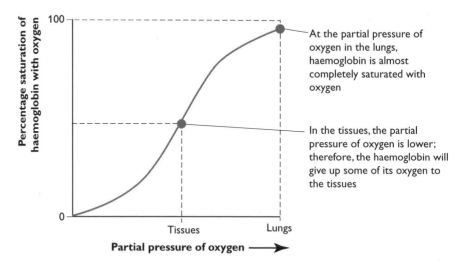

During exercise, there is an increased demand for oxygen. Exercise creates conditions that cause haemoglobin to release some of its oxygen more readily. These conditions are:

- a decrease in the partial pressure of oxygen in the muscle, which increases the oxygen diffusion gradient
- an increase in temperature in the blood and muscle
- an increase in carbon dioxide in the muscle, which increases the carbon dioxide diffusion gradient
- an increase in acidity (lower pH)

Control of ventilation

Breathing is controlled by the nervous system, which automatically causes an increase or decrease in the rate, depth and rhythm of breathing.

Exercise results in changes in the body that are detected by receptors:
- Chemoreceptors detect changes in blood acidity.
- Baroreceptors detect changes in blood pressure.
- Proprioreceptors detect extra movement caused by exercise.
- Stretch receptors prevent over inflation of the lungs.

Impulses from chemoreceptors and baroreceptors are detected by the inspiratory cells of the respiratory centre in the medulla oblongata.

Excessive stretching results in impulses being sent to the expiratory cells of the respiratory centre in the medulla oblongata of the brain, which then sends impulses that induce expiration. This is called the Hering–Breuer reflex.

The control of ventilation is summarised in the diagram below.

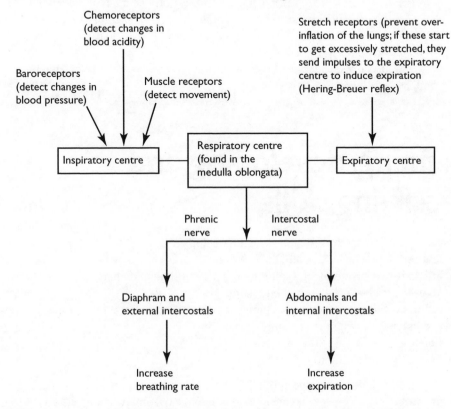

Altitude and the respiratory system

During exercise, more oxygen is required by the muscles for aerobic respiration. At high altitude (above 1500 m), there is less air and therefore less oxygen. This lower partial pressure of oxygen has the effect of decreasing the efficiency of respiration. This means the muscles do not receive as much oxygen because the haemoglobin cannot be fully saturated, which affects performance. If the haemoglobin carries less oxygen, there will be a reduction in the amount of oxygen available to the muscles, which will decrease aerobic performance.

The body adapts to high altitude by increasing the levels of red blood cells and haemoglobin. This means that after training at altitude, an athlete returning to sea level will have extra available energy for performance, thus delaying the onset of muscular fatigue.

What the examiner will expect you to be able to do

- You will be expected to be specific about the muscles involved in breathing: *external* intercostals are responsible for inspiration and *internal* intercostals for expiration. 'Intercostals' is not normally an acceptable answer.
- You might be required to calculate specific lung volumes, so make sure you take a calculator into the exam.
- Questions on neural control often ask how an increase in carbon dioxide affects breathing.

Defining, developing and classifying skills

A skilful performance has the following characteristics:
- **learned** — practice of a skill 'makes perfect'
- **efficient and economical** — minimum outlay of time and energy
- **goal-directed** — pre-determined results
- **follows a technical model** — a perfect demonstration of coaching points
- **consistent** — maximum certainty of success
- **fluent** — movements flow together
- **aesthetic** — pleasing to the eye

The types of skill that are important in PE are:
- **cognitive** — a skill involving the mental or intellectual ability of the performer (e.g. tactically outwitting an opponent in a long-distance race)
- **perceptual** — a skill involving the detection and interpretation of information (e.g. deciding where to pass the ball in soccer or if weather conditions might affect play)
- **motor** — a skill that involves movement and muscular control (e.g. swimming lengths)
- **perceptual/psychomotor** — this involves the cognitive, perceptual and motor aspects of skill (e.g. in a match situation, deciding who to pass to in soccer, and when and where to make the pass, and then actually making the pass)

Analysis of movement skills

Movement skills usually have several parts that are referred to as sub-routines. For example, in the front crawl swimming stroke, the sub-routines are body position, arm action, leg action and breathing.

A **continuum** (plural continua) is an imaginary scale between two extremes to show a gradual increase or decrease in characteristic. There are six continua you need to know and understand so that you can then apply them practically in order to classify different sports skills.

Continua used to classify skills

The six continua used to classify skills are:
- **environmental influence** — open–closed
- **pacing** — external–self
- **organisation** — low–high
- **task difficulty** — simple–complex
- **continuity** — discrete–serial–continuous
- **muscular involvement** — gross–fine

Environmental influence

Movement skills are affected by an **open environment** because the environment is always changing (e.g. the positions of opponents and team mates). There is much instant decision making (e.g. in invasion game situations). Skills are usually externally paced and are not predominantly habitual.

In a **closed environment**, skills are unaffected by the environment, which is predictable. They are habitual and follow a precise, well-practised technical model (e.g. a vault in gymnastics). They are usually self-paced, i.e. the performer has control.

Pacing

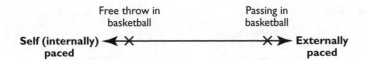

If a movement is **self-paced**, the performer is in control and determines when the movement starts and the rate at which it proceeds (e.g. a free throw in basketball).

If a movement is **externally paced**, control of the movement is not determined by the performer but by the environment (e.g. by the opponent(s), when passing in basketball).

Organisation

Movement skills with **low organisation** are made up of sub-routines (i.e. parts of a skill) that can be separated easily and practised on their own (e.g. swimming strokes).

Movement skills requiring **high organisation** have sub-routines that are very difficult to separate without disrupting the skill (e.g. a golf swing driving the ball off the tee).

Task difficulty

Forward roll/   Passing sequence in
sprinting   netball/tennis Serve

Simple ◄─✗──────────────────✗─► **Complex**

In a **simple task** there is limited information to process and there are few decisions to make. A small number of sub-routines are involved in which speed and timing are not critical (e.g. sprinting in athletics). The use of feedback is not significant.

In a **difficult task** there are high perceptual demands and much decision-making is required. There are many sub-routines involved in which speed and timing are critical (e.g. a tennis serve). The use of feedback is significant.

Continuity

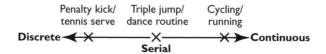

Penalty kick/   Triple jump/   Cycling/
tennis serve   dance routine   running

Discrete ◄─✗──────✗──────✗─► **Continuous**
                    Serial

Discrete skills have a clear, distinct beginning and end. To be repeated, the skill must be started again (e.g. taking a penalty kick in football and rugby).

Serial skills have several discrete elements that are put together in a particular order to make a sequence or compound skill (e.g. the triple jump or a floor routine in gymnastics)

Continuous skills have no clear beginning or end. The same skill or movement is repeated (e.g. cycling).

Muscular involvement

Shot put/   Darts/
rugby tackle   pistol shot

Gross ◄─✗──────────────✗─► **Fine**

Gross motor skills involve the movement of large muscles (e.g. shot put and weight-lifting).

Fine motor skills involve precise, intricate movements using small muscle groups. The emphasis is on hand–eye coordination (e.g. darts).

Examples of continua used to classify skills

A **javelin throw** is:
- closed, because the environment does not change
- self-paced, because the athlete starts when ready
- gross, because it is an explosive movement and rest is required between throws
- discrete, because it has a clear beginning and an end

A **swimming race start** is:
- discrete, because it has a clear, distinct beginning and end
- externally paced, because swimmers react to the stimulus of the gun
- a whole skill, because it cannot be broken down into sub-parts
- closed, because only one response movement is appropriate to the single stimulus presented. The environment is therefore constant.

The application of classification of skills in the organisation and determination of practice

Classifying skills helps PE teachers and coaches, because it tells them how to:
- teach skills
- improve skills
- practise skills to optimise performance

Before deciding on the type of practice, the coach or teacher should first classify the skill. Does the skill to be learned contain:
- several integrated actions? If so, it is a serial skill.
- a single integrated action? If so, it is a discrete skill.
- cyclical action? If so, it is a continuous skill.
- perceptual requirements? If so, it is an open skill.
- stereotyped movements? If so, it is a closed skill because the environment is constant/unchanged.

The teacher or coach then has to decide how to organise practice. Does the movement to be learned involve:
- skills that can be broken into parts? If so, it is a low-organisation skill.
- skills that cannot be broken into separate parts? If so, it is a high organisation skill.
- fine, intricate and perceptual skills? If so, it is a complex skill.
- gross, habitual or ballistic skills? If so, it is a simple skill.

Practice types and key terms explained in relation to sporting examples

Varied practice
In varied practice, the environment is continually changing. Therefore, varied practice is best for open skills. An example is three-versus-one 'keep ball' in netball or football.

Points about varied practice include the following:
- It improves positional play and passing technique in a realistic game situation.
- Opportunities arise for decision-making and the development of perceptual skills.
- Performers learn to adapt techniques to respond to an ever-changing environment.

- Adaptations are stored and, therefore, the experience (or schema) of the novice performer is expanded.
- It improves selective attention. This is the ability to pick out and focus on relevant parts of the display.
- It develops the skill of detecting warning signals (the cues before the major environmental ones), making information processing (the decision-making process) faster and more efficient.

Fixed practice

In fixed practice, the skills performed remain the same or repetitive. The environment does not change. Fixed practice is best for 'closed skills' that need to be 'over-learned' and well grooved (e.g. how to vault in gymnastics, skill drills or repetitive practices).

Fixed practice can be used because:
- the environment in which a closed skill is performed remains the same
- once perfected, the movement pattern does not change

Body movements that never change are known as **stereotyped actions**. They should be well groomed to the point at which they become habitual.

Part practice

For more complex movements, part practice allows confidence, motivation and under-standing to build up gradually. Part practice involves working on an isolated sub-routine to try to perfect it. It is best for skills that are low in organisation, and which can be broken down easily into separate sub-routines.

Points about part practice include the following:
- It can reduce fatigue in physically demanding skills. For example, the throwing phase in discus could be the focus of teaching and allow the learner to concentrate on this one area.
- It is useful in reducing overload (e.g. for a novice performer).
- It is useful when a task is complex or dangerous.
- Some skills can be taught by reversing the part order. For example, for shot put, the order of teaching would be:
  - throw and release
  - travel and trunk position
  - initial preparation
  - stance
  - grip
  This is called **backward chaining**.

Whole practice

Whole practice is best for skills that are high in organisation. An example is dribbling a ball in hockey. This does not easily break down into separate sub-routines.

Some points about whole practice include the following:
- It is the ideal model for all movements as it allows the learner to experience the feel of the skill (kinaesthesis).

- It is best for simple, discrete skills where a single, complete action is required.
- It wastes no time in assembling parts.
- Transfer to 'real situations' from practice is likely to be positive.

Whole–part–whole practice

Whole–part–whole practice allows the performer to get the feel of the movement. Using swimming as an example:

- This type of practice initially involves the presentation of the whole motor programme, i.e. an entire swimming stroke.
- Then, by introducing a float as a mechanical aid, practice focuses on a part of the skill, such as the leg kick.
- Finally, the whole stroke is reintroduced. The leg kick should have improved as a result of isolating it, giving relevant drills, teaching points and feedback to swimmers.

Ability and how it differs from skill

The words 'skill' and 'ability' are often used to mean the same thing. However, they are different terms with different characteristics.

Abilities are:

- innate, stable and enduring qualities that support many skills
- general — not specific

The characteristics of skill and ability are summarised in the table below.

Characteristic of skill	Characteristic of ability	Explanation
A movement that is learned	Innate (inherited)	Inborn abilities are determined by the genes inherited from our parents
Can be modified with practice	Stable, enduring proficiency	Abilities tend to remain unchanged
Depends on several abilities	Supports many skills	Each skill usually needs several supporting abilities in order to be well-learned

Tip Condensing information into a table can be an effective method of revision.

Types of ability

You need to understand and be able to give examples of two types of ability:

- **Gross motor abilities** involve physical proficiency abilities or movements and link to physical fitness. For example, explosive strength involves the effective use of energy for a short burst of effort, as in a rugby union tackle or line-out jump.
- **Perceptual** or **psychomotor abilities** involve information processing and decision making and then putting these decisions into action via movements. For example, being able to make rapid arm and hand movements that involve objects at speed, such as catching a ball as a slip fielder in cricket.

Development of motor skills

There are several key stages that the development of motor skills goes through:

- **Young children** (2–4 years old) use their abilities to learn **basic movement skills**, such as walking, running and balancing, which form the basis for further development.
- Children in the **early primary school years** (4–9 years old) are mentally and physically capable of learning skills. They are highly motivated and enthusiastic and require expert teaching to develop their basic movement skills into **fundamental motor skills**. Each fundamental motor skill has sub-routines against which success can be measured. There are clearly defined coaching points to ensure children learn the skills — such as catching, kicking and throwing — correctly. It is thought that abilities can be developed during early childhood, so it is important that, during this period, children are exposed to a wide range of experiences and are given the chance to practise. To enhance their skills, expert coaching is required, together with the support of family and friends who may be suitable role models.
- **Sport-specific skills** develop from fundamental motor skills by adapting and practising each skill so that it matches the requirements of the particular sport, such as catching a cricket ball, rugby ball or netball.

What the examiner will expect you to be able to do

- The difference between skill and ability is often asked in examination questions. You will be expected to be able to identify the supporting or 'underpinning' abilities for different activities. For example, gymnasts need strength, balance, coordination and flexibility. The questions sometimes ask for explanations of how abilities are developed during childhood. Possibilities include giving children a wide range of experiences and opportunities to practise, while receiving expert teaching or coaching.
- You will be expected to apply knowledge of different practice conditions to practical sporting examples and stages of learning.
- You should ensure you know at least *three* different characteristics of skill (e.g. consistent, learned and aesthetic).
- If you are asked to 'classify a skill', it is important that you can *explain* and *justify* how you have arrived at your decision. This is because the skill will differ depending on the situation in which it is performed. You will be required to explain this, together with characteristics of the skill that are relevant to the classification system you have chosen.
- Make sure that you can list and explain the key characteristics of skilful performers. Relating them to your favourite sporting activity might help you to remember them.

Information processing during skills performance

Models of information processing

Stages of information processing

The three main stages of information processing, in order, are:

stimulus identification ⟶ response selection ⟶ response programming

- **Stimulus identification** — detecting that there is a stimulus (information) and then interpreting the information. For example, detecting that there is a ball coming and then determining its speed, height and direction.
- **Response selection** — having interpreted the information (speed, height and direction of the ball), deciding what to do. In this example, deciding in which direction to move and which limb to re-position.
- **Response programming** — the information is sent via the nervous system to the appropriate muscles, so that the appropriate movement can be carried out.

Key processes in information processing

The improvement in performance of a skill can be related to various key processes involved in information processing. In order, these are:

display ⟶ sensory ⟶ perception ⟶ memory ⟶ decision making ⟶ effector mechanism ⟶ feedback

- **Display** — the surroundings or environment of the performer. For example, for a footballer, display includes the ball, team mates, opponents, spectators, the referee and the coach or teacher.
- **Sensory input** — the senses detect information and receptors are stimulated. The senses involved are vision, hearing and **proprioception**. Proprioception is the sense that allows us to know the position of our bodies and what our muscles and joints are doing, and to feel objects involved in our performance (e.g. the ball or hockey stick). Proprioceptive sense consists of **touch**, **kinaesthesis** and **equilibrium**.
- **Perception** — the process that interprets and makes sense of the information received. It consists of three elements:
  - **detection** — detecting that the stimulus is present
  - **comparison** — comparing the stimulus to stimuli present in the long-term memory
  - **recognition** — matching the stimulus to one found in long-term memory
- **Memory** — important in both perceptual and decision-making processes. It consists of **short-term sensory stores** (STSS), **short-term memory** (STM) and **long-term memory** (LTM). (See page 44 for further explanation of these terms.)

- **Decision making** — the translatory mechanism. Once the information has been interpreted, the correct response has to be put into action. This will be in the form of a **motor programme**.
- **Effector mechanism** — the motor programme is put into action by sending impulses through the nervous system to the appropriate muscles, enabling them to carry out the required actions.
- **Feedback** — once the motor programme has been put into action, the display changes and new information is created. This new information is known as feedback.

It is important to show that you understand terms such as perception, translation (decision-making) and effective control by being able to link them with appropriate sporting activities.

For example, in volleyball:
- **perception** involves making sense of incoming information, i.e. using selective attention in order to see the stimulus of the ball leaving the hand of the opposing server.
- **translation** is deciding what is happening and what action to take through the interaction of short-term and long-term memory. For example: 'with the ball at chest height, I will use a set volley'.
- **effector control** is carrying out the movement (e.g. hands high, 'viewfinder').

Whiting's model of information processing for perceptual motor performance

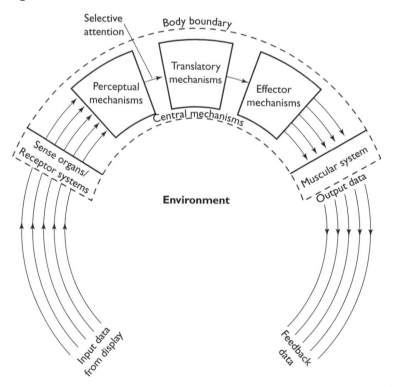

content guidance

An important point to note about this model is that it shows five arrows entering the perceptual mechanism and only one leaving. This process is called selective attention. It allows unnecessary information to be filtered out and helps us to focus on relevant information in a system of 'limited capacity'.

Other points to note are as follows:
- Input comes from the display, i.e. the sporting environment.
- Specific parts of the display stimulate the sense organs and, therefore, pass to the receptors.
- The translatory mechanisms recognise the input and decisions are made about what action to take.
- The effector mechanisms send impulses to the muscular system so that the movement can be carried out.
- An action is performed (output data).
- Feedback is required for accurate performance.

Welford's model of information processing

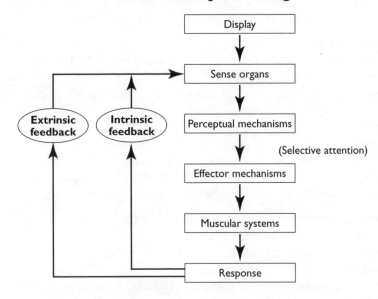

According to this model:
- **display** is the sporting environment from which information is selected.
- **sense organs** are responsible for picking up important information from the display.
- **perceptual mechanisms** decide on the appropriate response.
- **effector mechanisms and muscular systems** carry out movements once decisions have been made.
- **extrinsic feedback** is feedback from a source outside the performer.
- **intrinsic feedback** is feedback from within the performer.

The memory process

Memory is important in:
- storing and retrieving information
- interpreting information by comparing it with that from a previous experience
- determining the motor programme to use to implement the action

Components of memory

Short-term sensory store

The features of the short-term sensory store (STSS) are as follows:
- All information is held for a very short time (0.25–1 second).
- Capacity is limitless within the brief time available.
- Important information is attended to (selective attention); that which is not important is ignored and eventually lost and replaced by new information.
- The perceptual mechanism determines important information (recognition aspect of perception).
- Input from the STSS goes into the short-term memory (STM).

Short-term memory

Short-term memory (STM) is referred to as **working memory**. The features of STM are as follows:
- Information is compared with that which has been previously learned (comparison aspect of perception).
- Information is only stored for up to a minute or so, unless it is rehearsed or repeated.
- It has limited capacity — 7±2 pieces of information.
- Capacity can be increased by '**chunking**' with other information (see page 45).
- It is responsible for the execution of the motor programme.

Long-term memory

The features of long-term memory (LTM) are as follows:
- It stores information that has been well-learned and practised.
- It has a very large/unlimited capacity.
- After much practise, motor programmes are stored in the LTM.
- Stored information is retrieved and compared with new information — this is the recognition aspect of perception.

Strategies to improve retention and retrieval

There are a number of strategies that can be applied to help store and remember information:
- **Rehearsal and practice** — frequently practising and rehearsing the skill stores the motor programme. It also creates a memory trace, by carrying the skill image to-and-fro between the short-term and long-term memories.

- **Association/linking** — linking new information with that already known. For example, the sports-specific skill of catching a cricket ball is linked to the fundamental motor skill of catching.
- **Simplicity** — learners should be allowed time to take in new information, which should be kept as simple as possible. More complex details can be added later. Similar types of information or skill should not be presented too close together. For example, a swimming teacher should concentrate on one stroke at a time.
- **Organisation** — information should be organised and presented in a meaningful way. For example, a gymnastic or trampolining sequence should be learned by practising the individual movements in the order in which they appear.
- **Chunking** — linking information together allows more information to be dealt with at the same time. Experienced performers can look at the whole field of play. Coaches should avoid giving too much information at a time.
- **Uniqueness** — presenting information in an unusual way makes it more likely to be remembered.
- **Positive reinforcement** — if learners receive praise and encouragement, the information is more likely to be remembered. This requires frequent feedback.
- **Interesting/enjoyable** — if learners enjoy the experience, the possibility of it being remembered increases.
- **Meaningful** — if learners appreciate the relevance of the skill to their performance, they are more likely to remember it.
- **Imagery** — if learners have a mental image of the skill, they are more likely to remember it. This is why demonstrations are important.

Tip To help you remember the above, it would be a good idea to convert this information into another format, such as a spider diagram, with links to practical examples.

Reaction time

Key terms

- **Reaction time** is the time from the stimulus occurring to the performer starting to move in response to it
- **Movement time** is the time taken from starting the movement to completing it
- **Response time** is the time from the onset of the stimulus to the completion of the movement

Using the 100 metres sprint as an example:

starter's gun goes off ⟶ sprinter pushes on blocks = reaction time

sprinter pushing on blocks ⟶ sprinter crossing finish line = movement time

starter's gun goes off ⟶ sprinter crosses finish line = response time

A further sporting example to aid your understanding of reaction time, movement time and response time can be taken from tennis. Top-class professional tennis players serve at very high speeds. Suppose that it takes:

- 0.17 seconds for the ball to reach the receiver once it has left the server's racket
- 0.15 seconds for the receiver to decide on an action
- 0.20 seconds for the receiver to play a return, having decided on the stroke to play

From these data, the receiver's reaction, movement and response times can be calculated as:

reaction time = 0.15 seconds

movement time = 0.20 seconds

response time = 0.35 seconds

Factors affecting reaction time

There are a number of factors that affect reaction time. They include:
- **age** — reaction and response times decrease with age up to a certain point, and then increase
- **gender** — males have shorter response times than females, but differences lessen with age
- **arousal** — optimum levels of arousal are needed for a quick reaction (note that drugs may affect this)
- the **sensory system** used — kinaesthesis is quickest, sight slowest
- the **limb** used — feet are slower than hands and the preferred side is usually quicker
- **personality** — extroverts react more quickly than introverts

Reaction time can also be affected by external factors, including:
- a warning. If a warning is given, it helps to prepare the athlete. An example is 'set' at the start of a sprint.
- the intensity of stimulus. For example, using an orange ball when playing football in the snow helps players to pick it out from the background.
- the likelihood of the stimulus occurring. If the stimulus has a good chance of happening, the reaction will be quicker.

Simple and choice reaction times

Simple reaction time is the time taken for a sports performer to react to a **single stimulus**.

Choice reaction time occurs when there is more than one stimulus and/or more than one response. It occurs in many sporting situations. When there are more choices and decisions to be made, reaction times lengthen.

Hicks's law

Hicks's law states that choice reaction time *increases linearly* with the number of stimulus and choice alternatives. For example, if there is double the choice, the reaction time doubles.

Hicks's law has important implications for sports performers, who should try to:

- disguise their intentions, therefore increasing the number of possible alternatives that opponents have to select from. This increases the reaction times of the opponents.
- pick up 'cues' about the intended response of their opponents. This reduces the number of alternatives and reaction times are reduced.

Ways to improve the response time of a performer

There are a number of ways in which teachers and coaches can try to improve (reduce) the response time of a performer. These include:

- improving **physical fitness**
- **practice** — the more a stimulus is responded to, the shorter the reaction time becomes. Practising sprint starts is a suitable example.
- **stimulus–response compatibility** — if the response is the one that would normally be made, it will be quicker than otherwise. Practising the marking of set plays in a team game, such as football, is a suitable example.
- **mental rehearsal** — going over responses in the mind ensures that the performer attends to the correct cues and expects and responds to appropriate stimuli. This works on the neuromuscular system and is important in complex tasks that have a lot of information processing, such as passing in hockey.
- **experience** — carrying out the activity enhances awareness of the probability of the stimulus occurring. Practising passing in netball is a suitable example.
- **warm-up** — this ensures that the cardiorespiratory, vascular and neuromuscular systems are adequately prepared
- the correct level of **arousal/motivation** — this ensures that performers are at their optimum levels of arousal
- **concentration/selective attention** — getting the performer to concentrate and focus on the relevant stimulus and ignore everything else. This is particularly important in simple reaction time situations.
- good **anticipation**
  - spatial anticipation involves predicting what will happen. A batsman anticipating a fast bowler's slower ball is a suitable example.
  - temporal anticipation involves predicting when it will happen. Athletes anticipating when the gun will go off in a sprint start is a suitable example.
- **early cue detection** — analysing the opponent's play in order to anticipate what he or she intends to do. Analysing the opponent's short and long serves in badminton is a suitable example.

Tip To help you remember the above, it would be a good idea to convert this information into another format, such as a spider diagram, with links to practical examples.

Psychological refractory period

This is the negative side of anticipation. If we anticipate something wrongly, then our reactions are slower. If we detect a stimulus and are processing that information when a second stimulus arrives, we cannot attend to the second stimulus until we have finished processing the first. Therefore, humans can only deal with one piece of information at a time (the single-channel hypothesis). This delay in processing information increases reaction time. The delay is called the **psychological refractory period** (PRP).

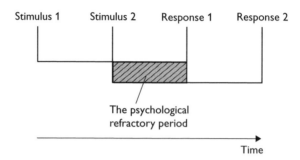

The PRP is the delay caused by being able to process only one piece of information at a time. An example of its importance is in games such as rugby, when 'dummying' an opponent. An opponent who 'buys the dummy' is still reacting to it when the second stimulus of carrying on without releasing the ball is received. Deception makes use of the PRP by creating uncertainty and insecurity in sports performers.

Feedback

Feedback is the information received by the performer during the course of the movement or as a result of it. There are several different types of feedback of which you need to be aware. These are summarised in the tables below.

Intrinsic feedback	Extrinsic feedback
Comes from within (e.g. proprioceptors and kinaesthesis)	Comes from external sources (e.g. teacher or coach)
Concerns the feel of the movement (e.g. the feel of balance during a handstand)	Received via sight and hearing and is used to support intrinsic feedback
Very important for experienced performers Novices need to be made aware of the need to develop this form of feedback	Important for beginners who are often reliant on it if they wish to improve

Concurrent (continuous) feedback	Terminal feedback
Intrinsic	Extrinsic
Received during the movement and generated by the proprioceptors or kinaesthesis (e.g. gymnasts knowing they are balanced correctly)	Given after the movement is completed or later (e.g. a coach discussing the match and summarising the performance at the next training session)

Positive feedback	Negative feedback
Movement is successful and feedback reinforces the learning	Movement is incorrect or unsuccessful and feedback is used to make it successful (i.e. error correction)
Can be intrinsic or extrinsic (e.g. positive extrinsic feedback is when a badminton coach praises players when they serve correctly); this can motivate the performers to succeed	Can be intrinsic or extrinsic (e.g. negative intrinsic feedback is when advanced-level performers detect or 'feel' an error in movement and then try to correct it themselves)

Knowledge of performance (KP)	Knowledge of results (KR)
Concerns the quality of movement	Concerns the outcome of movement
Could be from discussing the performance or watching a video	Usually arises from teachers or coaches seeing the result (e.g. watching the movement on video)
Can be external (from teachers or coaches) or internal (from proprioceptors and kinaesthesis)	Extrinsic Can be positive or negative
Important for experienced performers	Very important in the early stages of learning and for improving performance

Why is feedback important?

Feedback is important because:
- performers know what to do in order to improve
- correct actions are reinforced
- incorrect actions are stopped and bad habits are prevented
- performers are motivated and their confidence is boosted

In order for feedback to be effective, it should:
- make comparisons with previous performances
- be specific to the performance
- be easily understood by performers
- be in manageable amounts
- be linked to goals
- be immediate, so that it remains firmly in the memory

What the examiner will expect you to be able to do

- Questions may require you to explain how feedback differs as performers move through the stages of learning, i.e. from the associative phase to the autonomous phase:
  - At the associative phase, performers begin to monitor their own feedback, but extrinsic feedback from a coach is still needed.

– At the autonomous phase, performers become less reliant on KR (knowledge of results), and are better at detecting their own errors through
intrinsic feedback. Performers are able to correct their own performance.
- Questions on information processing are often about one of the information-processing models. A useful approach is to try to draw the model or
use the diagram provided to explain each part sequentially. Practical
examples to illustrate your understanding should be used at each stage.
- Questions on the memory process may require you to name some of the
features of the various storage parts of the memory. For example, the long-
term memory is said to have limitless capacity, to last a lifetime and to store
motor programmes. It is important to read the questions carefully and give
accurate answers (e.g. make sure that you do not confuse the short-term
sensory store with the short-term memory).
- You need to be able to define reaction time, movement time and response
time and relate these to sporting examples. These are regularly asked for
in the examination.
- Feedback is referred to as 'an aid to performance' and you are often asked
to 'state its benefits'. Answers should include building confidence, providing
motivation and correcting errors.

Control of motor skills
Motor programmes

A motor programme is a set of movements stored in the long-term memory, which
specifies the components of a skill.

Key points

- Motor skills are physical actions.
- Control involves the manipulation and adjustment of movement to produce the
required skill.
- A motor programme or executive motor programme (EMP) is an overall plan of
the whole skill or pattern of movement.
- The plan is stored in the long-term memory (LTM).
- The EMP comprises sub-routines — mini skills often performed in sequence, which,
collectively, make up the whole skill.
- Sub-routines appear to be performed fluently and automatically when the skill has
been grooved or over-learned.
- Automatic execution of the skill takes place when the performer is at the expert stage.
- An expert is said to be at the autonomous phase of learning.

The organisation of a skill can be **hierarchical** and **sequential**. Hierarchical means in order of importance — the EMP is more important than the supporting sub-routines. Sequential means that sub-routines are often performed in a particular order. In the diagram below this is applied to a tennis serve, which is low in organisation. Note how the sub-routines are performed in sequence to make up the EMP.

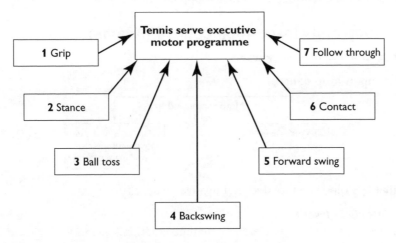

Low-organisation skills

If a skill is low in organisation (e.g. throwing the javelin), it can be divided easily into sub-routines that can be taught and practised separately.

You need to know three practice methods that can be used for a skill of low organisation. These are:

- **part practice** — each sub-routine is learned separately and in isolation
- **progressive part practice** — two sub-routines are taught separately and then practised together before teaching a third sub-routine in isolation. The combination of three sub-routines is then practised as one skill.
- **whole–part–whole** — the skill is practised as a whole. One sub-routine is taken out and practised separately. The skill is then performed as a whole.

Sub-routines, particularly in throwing skills, can often be taught in reverse order. This practice method is called **backward chaining**.

High-organisation skills

If a skill is high in organisation, it cannot be divided into sub-routines. A single sub-routine cannot be taught as an isolated component.

You need to know two practice methods that can be used for a skill of high organisation. These are:

- **whole practice** — the skill is performed as a whole (e.g. dribbling a football)
- **task simplification** — making the task easier than it really is. For example, short tennis simplifies the rudiments of the major game of tennis.

Motor control

Motor control involves manipulation and often adjustment of the body during performance in order to bring about the desired response. The control of motor skills is explained by the **open-loop** and **closed-loop** theories.

Open-loop and closed-loop control (Adams)

Motor control occurs at three levels.

Level 1: open-loop control

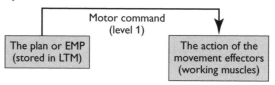

Note that open-loop control does not involve feedback.

Key points about level 1
- The EMP is stored as an overall plan in the long-term memory.
- The EMP is triggered by the 'situation' and is transferred almost spontaneously to the working muscle.
- The open loop is termed the **memory trace** and is responsible for starting the action.
- The function is to produce the initial movement of the skill and no reference is made to feedback.
- For a skill of rapid execution, such as a golf drive, the movement is so rapid that feedback cannot be referenced after the swing has started.

Levels 2 and 3: closed-loop control

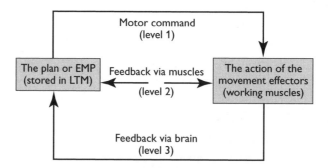

Note that levels 2 and 3 involve feedback. Feedback completes or closes the loop.

Key points about level 2
- It operates on a short feedback loop and is a closed loop system of control.
- Control is achieved through muscle reaction.

- Without thinking, rapid adjustments can be made during performance. For example, gymnasts make subconscious alterations in order to retain balance during their routines.
- Adjustments are stored in the long-term memory.
- It does not engage the central cognitive process.
- Its function is to complete the skill.

Key points about level 3
- It operates on a longer feedback loop because information is relayed to the brain, which in turn processes modifications to performance.
- Feedback is information about the performance and outcome of the skill.
- It involves thought and greater attention is given to the plan.
- Adjustments are stored in the long-term memory as fresh motor programmes.
- It is called the **perceptual trace** and is frequently used in open skills that require decision making (e.g. passing a ball in netball or hockey).
- Its function is to complete the skill.

Perceptual trace
During performance, the perceptual trace compares the current action with the learned pattern of movement, which is stored in the long-term memory. If the comparison matches, the skill is allowed to continue and is reinforced. If a mismatch is detected, the action will be modified. Modifications are stored as fresh motor programmes.

Drawbacks of open-loop and closed-loop theories
- It is not possible to store the large number of motor programmes as separate memory traces for every movement in long-term memory. This gives an information retention problem.
- If it was possible to retain an infinite number of motor programmes, it would be difficult for the memory trace to retrieve or recall the required plan in sufficient time to execute the skill.
- Sport contains many unusual/spontaneous actions. These are creative actions we often see in 'open skills' and are called 'novel responses'. If the relevant motor programme has not been set up in long-term memory, the action of the novel response cannot be explained by this theory.

Schema theory (Schmidt)

Schema theory provides a solution to the problems of the open-loop and closed-loop theories. It states that EMPs are not stored as separate plans (as presented by open-loop and closed-loop theories), but are stored in the long-term memory as experiences or relationships with motor programmes or movements. These relationships are termed 'generalised movements' and they allow performers to adapt quickly in response to a given situation.

Key points
- A schema is an accumulation of experiences.
- Stored information helps in decision making.

- Experiences or relationships are termed generalised movements.
- Generalised movements are adaptations or modifications of movements that are transferred to aid learning and performance of other skills.
- Experience can be adapted and used to meet the demands of a new situation.
- The process of using previous experience to assist with learning new skills, and with the performance of over-learned skills, is called 'transfer'.
- Schema theory supports variability of practice.

Experience is accumulated by gathering information from four sources of information or memory items. Using the example of two attackers approaching one defender in rugby, these memory items are identified and explained in the table below. The example relates *specifically* to the ball carrier.

Type of schema	Functions	Memory items stored each time a movement is performed	Explanation of memory items using a practical example
Recall	To store information	(1) Knowledge of initial conditions and desired outcome	Refers to the environmental situation (e.g. the player may have experienced a similar situation in a practice or previous game)
	To start the response	(2) Knowledge of response specification	Refers to knowing what to do (e.g. the well-timed pass may be the answer as it has been successful in similar situations)
Recognition	To control the movement	(3) Knowledge of sensory consequences (actual feedback)	Refers to kinaesthesis — how much pressure or force to apply to the skill (e.g. how hard the ball should be passed)
	To evaluate the performance	(4) Knowledge of outcome/KR	Refers to knowing what the result is likely to be (e.g. the well-timed pass makes it impossible for the defender to make a tackle. What was the result?)

Ways in which coaches can organise practices to enable schemata to develop include the following:
- Training should be varied and should:
  - include lots of information
  - be as realistic as possible (e.g. game situations)
  - include transferable elements
  - include lots of feedback
- Terminal feedback should be provided to strengthen the schema in the memory.

What the examiner will expect you to be able to do

- You need to be able to differentiate between the benefits of a motor programme, in terms of the efficient, quick reactions it can produce, and the ways in which it is developed through feedback and practice. You could be asked to name some sub-routines of a skill and to explain how a basic motor programme can develop into a more complex one by fine-tuning the performance through specific practice.
- A question on closed-loop control will require you to use a sporting example to help explain how errors are detected and amended by feedback.
- You will be expected to know the four parts of the schema theory outlined in the table on page 55, so that you can recall and apply them to sporting examples in any questions set on this topic area.

Learning skills
Theories related to learning movement skills

Connectionist or associationist theories

Connectionist theories depend upon linking (connecting) a **stimulus** to a **response**. This connection is often termed a **learning bond** or **S–R bond**, where 'S' represents a stimulus (or cue) and 'R' represents the response to this cue. The S–R bond is stored in the long-term memory. The connection of the S–R bond is strengthened by **reinforcement** — the process that causes behaviour to recur.

A practical example is a ball high in the air acting as a stimulus for a tennis player. The response to the stimulus is to hit the ball. If successful, the response connects with the stimulus and a learning bond is formed. If the response is ineffective, the S–R bond is weakened. (This is trial-and-error learning.)

Reinforcement can be given in two ways:
- **Positive reinforcement** involves the presentation of the stimulus of approval or a 'satisfier'. This could be in the form of verbal praise or a tangible reward. The aim is to encourage the correct action in the future.
- **Negative reinforcement** involves the withdrawal of praise offered for the correct response, or the use of punishment (e.g. extra training) for an incorrect response.

Thorndike's laws
Although learning can take place in various ways, the psychologist Thorndike believed that the most effective way to learn is to form and strengthen a learning bond through

the application of reinforcement. Thorndike put forward three laws relating to the application of reinforcement.

- **Law of effect** — positive reinforcement increases the chance of behaviour reoccurring. (A coach should try to praise or reward performers when they are successful.)
- **Law of exercise** — the more often a response is reinforced, the stronger the learning bond will become.
- **Law of readiness** — learning by connecting can only take place when the nervous system has reached an appropriate stage of maturation.

Operant conditioning

Operant conditioning is a major connectionist theory put forward by the psychologist Skinner (1974). It is mainly concerned with responses rather than with stimuli.

There are a number of key points about operant conditioning that you need to know and be able to apply to a sports coaching situation. These include:

- manipulating or structuring a situation to bring about a desired response
- learning by trial and error
- reinforcing the response (e.g. positive comments)
- changing the response — a process termed 'behaviour shaping'
- the process of changing the response is termed 'behaviour shaping'

Cognitive learning theory

Cognitive theories emphasise the individual's thought processes as opposed to the influence of a stimulus and a response.

Key points

- **Gestalt theory** is the major cognitive theory.
- Cognitive psychologists Wertheimer and Köhler believed that learning is most effective through problem solving and that insight is a means of learning.
- This approach is in direct contrast to the connectionist belief.
- A cognitive process is a thinking process.
- Generally, learning a skill takes place quite slowly in the early stages and then quite rapidly later.

According to cognitive theory, for learning to occur, five factors must be in place:

- **Perception** — interpretation or understanding of the whole task. For example, difficulty encountered in the execution of a vault may be eased if the gymnast is made aware of, and understands, the mechanics of the movement.
- **Previous experience** — related experience can help to establish insight into how a new task is to be performed. For example, the experience of throwing a ball relates to learning to serve in tennis. This is transfer of learning.
- **Current knowledge** — the learner needs an insight into what is required — for example, the strategies required to defeat a full court press in basketball.
- **Motivation** — the learner must be motivated to solve the problem.
- **Self-esteem** — learning can be accomplished only if the novice has positive self-perception.

Applying cognitive theory therefore involves a period of purposeful experimentation in which the learner uses experience, knowledge and perception to solve the whole problem.

In practical terms, this means that skills are best learned by conditioning or by adapting games, rather than by perfecting techniques in isolation. For example, a Gestaltist would argue that short tennis is a better introduction to tennis than teaching separate shots. Mechanical guidance can be used to simplify the whole skill. For example, a tumbling harness can help the learning of a somersault in trampolining or a buoyancy aid can help the novice swimmer to experience the 'feeling of tone' of the whole stroke.

According to Gestalt theory, the solution to the whole problem may emerge suddenly. This is called the **eureka phenomenon**.

Observational learning

The psychologist Bandura believed that learning was most effectively achieved by imitating or copying others.

The theory of observational learning involves watching a demonstration and replicating the model. The learner must display four factors before learning can be achieved through observation. These factors are summarised in the table below.

Factor	Learner	Coach
Attention	Must focus concentration on the model	Can highlight the key areas of the skill
Retention	Must remember the image	Should give a clear, correct image so it can be remembered
Motor reproduction	Must have the necessary ability and skill to replicate the demonstration	Should make sure the performer is physically capable of performing the skill
Motivation	Must have the drive to learn	Can reward or praise the performer to create the drive to learn

Coaches can use Bandura's model of observational learning to help a performer to progress.

Phases of movement skill learning

The psychologists Fitts and Posner put forward the idea of three learning phases or stages, which relate directly to the acquisition of motor skills.

Learning phases

The cognitive phase
This is the thinking stage. The key points are as follows:
- The learner engages in mental rehearsal and benefits from observing a demonstration.

- By the end of this phase, the learner attempts to perform the skill.
- Feedback needs to be both extrinsic and positive, to highlight errors in performance.

The associative phase

This is the practice stage in which the learner participates physically. The key points are as follows:

- The response is inefficient and often incorrect.
- The learner requires great concentration during performance.
- Mental rehearsal can help learning and develop fluency.
- Demonstration remains important and reinforcement should be positive.
- Control of the skill is largely through external feedback (KR).
- The learner begins to use intrinsic or kinaesthetic feedback (KP) to control the skill.

The autonomous phase

This is the expert stage, at which the skill can be executed automatically. The key points are as follows:

- The movement has been 'grooved' or over-learned.
- The correct response can now be associated with the correct 'feeling tone'.
- Attention can be given to peripheral environmental cues.
- Demonstration and mental rehearsal remain important.
- The expert uses intrinsic feedback for self-correction (KP).
- Negative extrinsic feedback from the coach assists fault correction and helps in fine tuning.

Methods of guidance

There are four types of guidance that can be used to help the learning process:

- **Visual guidance** can be in the form of a precise demonstration showing the action or displaying changes. Chalking the ground during bowling practice in cricket to give the learner a target is an example. Visual guidance is best used at the cognitive stage of learning, as it registers an image for a longer time than other methods of guidance and can be easily absorbed by the learner.
- **Verbal guidance** involves telling the learner what to do. It is of more benefit for the learning of open skills that require decision-making and perceptual judgements. Verbal guidance is best used at the autonomous stage of learning and is less relevant to beginners.
- **Manual guidance** involves the coach holding and physically 'shaping' the body to give the learner an idea of how the skill should feel (e.g. learning a tennis serve).
- **Mechanical guidance** makes use of an object or piece of apparatus to shape the skill (e.g. a gymnastic harness).

Note that manual and mechanical guidance have some drawbacks associated with them. For example, they are not given in the 'real game' situation, so their overuse could result in negative transfer. There is also the risk that the learner becomes reliant on the type of guidance. They are of limited use in large group situations and with fast, complex movements. However, they can be used to give support or confidence in potentially dangerous situations.

Transfer of learning

Transfer is the process of one skill influencing the learning and performance of a separate skill. This is an important topic — practically all learning is based on some form of transfer.

You need to know about five types of transfer and to be able to apply them to practical examples:

- **Positive transfer** occurs when one skill helps the learning and performance of another — for example, two skills that have similar forms, such as a tennis serve and an overarm volleyball serve.
- **Negative transfer** is evident when one skill impairs the learning and performance of another. For example, the wrist actions in tennis and squash are completely different. A fixed wrist in tennis can have negative effects in squash, which requires a flexible wrist.
- **Proactive transfer** takes place when a previously learned skill influences the learning and performance of later skills, either positively or negatively. For example, learning to throw overarm as a child will later help the racquet arm action when learning to serve in tennis.
- **Retroactive transfer** occurs when new skills influence the learning and performance of old skills, either positively or negatively. For example, learning a tennis serve as a student could influence the throwing skills that were acquired in childhood.
- **Bilateral transfer** is the transfer of learning from limb to limb. An example would be a player with a dominant right foot learning to kick with the left.

To try to ensure that positive transfer takes place when teaching a sports skill, a coach can:

- ensure the two skills involved are sufficiently alike for transfer to occur
- practise or give experience of the original task
- provide realistic practice or game scenarios
- give a similar stimulus/response/movement pattern
- make the performer aware of the potential for transfer
- explain the mechanical principles or key elements behind the skill and ensure that the learner is involved in skill analysis

It is important that you are aware of the link between schema theory and transfer of learning. Schema is an accumulation of knowledge and motor programmes that can be adapted and transferred to help a response to a new situation.

Motivation and arousal

Motivation is the psychological wish, desire or drive to succeed and perform well in sport. **Arousal** is the degree of excitement or activation that prepares the person for performance.

Learning and performance of motor skills cannot take place without a degree of motivation.

Intrinsic motivation

Intrinsic motivation is inner drive and self-satisfaction (e.g. mastery for its own sake).

Advantages
- Longer lasting than extrinsic motivation
- Good for youngsters to place more emphasis on fun and enjoyment (etc.) than on trophies or praise

Disadvantages
- Less relevant in professional sport
- Difficult for some people to generate enough intrinsic motivation to continue participating in an activity

Extrinsic motivation

Extrinsic motivation is when motivation comes from an outside source such as praise from a coach or the possibility of an award or trophy. Extrinsic reward is a valuable motivator for a beginner, but will eventually undermine intrinsic motivation.

Advantages
- Material rewards increase the probability of a particular behaviour occurring again
- Motivates individuals to continue involvement

Disadvantages
- Overuse of extrinsic motivation can lead to a decrease in intrinsic motivation
- Rewards can transform what was regarded as a 'fun' activity into a chore

Motivation has two components:
- **Intensity of behaviour** is the degree of physical and emotional energy displayed by the individual. This is known as **arousal**.
- **Direction of behaviour** is the way arousal is used to reach a goal or target.

Drive theory

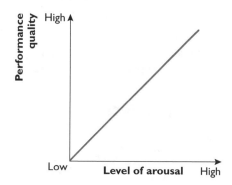

- Drive theory proposes that as arousal increases, there is a proportional increase in the quality of performance.
- The quality of performance depends upon how well the skill has been learned.
- Actions that have been learned are called dominant responses.
- Dominant responses are the actions that are most likely to occur as arousal increases.

Implications for teaching and learning
- In the associative phase of learning, the dominant response is likely to be incorrect. Therefore, the novice learns best when in a condition of low arousal.
- In the autonomous phase of learning, an expert performs better in an environment that stimulates high arousal.

The inverted-U theory

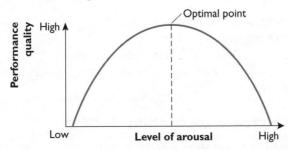

The inverted-U theory predicts that as arousal increases, the quality of performance and the capacity to concentrate improve and are at their best at the optimum point. The optimum point is also called the 'threshold of arousal'. It occurs midway along the arousal axis. After the optimal point, if arousal continues to increase, the capacity to perform and concentrate will decline.

Implications of under-arousal for teaching and learning
- The attention field (the environment of which we are aware) widens excessively.
- The learner is not able to selectively attend to the most relevant cues.
- An information overload will result.

Implications of over-arousal for teaching and learning
The attention field narrows excessively, causing relevant cues to be missed. In this condition, the learner may experience high anxiety or panic. The technical term for this condition is **hypervigilance**.

Optimal arousal
At optimal arousal:
- the attention field adjusts to the ideal width
- the learner is able to selectively attend to the relevant environmental cues and process information effectively (**cue utilisation**)
- concentration is at a maximum

Drive reduction theory

The initial drive to learn the skill is strong, but once the skill is learned, drive is reduced. As a result, the performance quality of the skill will decline.

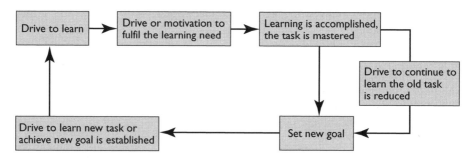

Implications for teaching and learning

- The drive to learn must be maintained.
- To replenish the drive, new targets should be introduced.
- Drive reduction could occur because of boredom through repetition.
- Practices should vary.

Strategies to increase motivation

Strategies to increase the motivation to learn include:

- positively reinforcing the learner's performance
- providing extrinsic rewards
- ensuring that learning targets are challenging and realistic
- appropriately changing the practice or drill to attain a specific goal (variability of practice)
- making use of role models
- presenting the skill as a worthwhile element to learn
- making the learner aware of how progressions can be made
- ensuring that practices are fun.

Practice conditions

Massed practice

Massed practice is a practice session with no breaks. It is used when the task is simple and discrete, and when motivation and ability of the group are high.

The advantages of massed practice are that:

- more physical work is possible in a single session
- it allows the learner to experience the flow of the whole skill
- it is good for the development of kinaesthesis

Distributed practice

Distributed practice includes breaks, so the session is divided into short periods. It is used when the task is complex and continuous, and the ability of the group is low. Distributed practice is more effective than massed practice in the learning of motor skills.

The advantages of distributed practice are that:
- it allows periods of rest
- feedback and performance analysis can be given
- it enables learners to engage in **mental rehearsal** to create a picture of the skill in their minds

What the examiner will expect you to be able to do

- You need to be able to describe the key characteristics of each of the three phases of learning. It is also important that you are able to differentiate between the cognitive phase of learning and the cognitive theory of learning, so that in the examination you do not misinterpret a question and give an answer that earns no marks.
- You should know the difference between positive and negative reinforcement — positive reinforcement involves a pleasant stimulus such as praise for a correct response; negative reinforcement means the withdrawal of approval when an undesired response prevails.
- It is important that you learn Thorndike's laws so that you are able to show how to make the S–R bond stronger. You will be expected to know the difference between positive and negative transfer and to be able to use appropriate examples to illustrate your understanding.
- Questions on motivation usually focus on either an explanation of the difference between extrinsic and intrinsic motivation or on the methods that could be used to motivate a sports performer. It is important that you show clear knowledge of these methods and that you can use examples from sport to illustrate them.

Questions & Answers

This section of the guide contains questions that are similar in style to those you can expect to see in Unit Test 2562. The questions cover the four areas of Section A and the four areas of Section B of Module 2562: **The Application of Physiological and Psychological Knowledge to Improve Performance**.

Each question is followed by an average or poor response (Candidate A) and an A-grade response (Candidate B).

You should try to answer these questions yourself, so that you can compare your answers with the candidates' responses. In this way, you should be able to identify your strengths and weaknesses in both subject knowledge and exam technique.

Examiner's comments

All candidate responses are followed by examiner's comments. These are preceded by the icon *e* and indicate where credit is due. In the weaker answers they point out areas for improvement, specific problems and common errors, such as vagueness, irrelevance and misinterpretation of the question.

Question 1

Muscle contraction

(a) There are different types of muscular contraction that a muscle can perform. The table below shows an example of concentric muscle action.

Action performed	Joint	Active muscle	Type of contraction	Muscle function
Biceps curl (upward phase)	Elbow	Biceps brachii	Concentric	Agonist

Using the biceps curl as an example and the same table headings, analyse another type of muscular contraction that takes place during this movement. (5 marks)

(b) Complete the movement analysis table below, by identifying A, B, C, D, E and F. (6 marks)

Joint	Joint type	Articulating bones	Movement produced	Agonist
Ankle	A:	Talus, tibia and fibula	Plantarflexion	B:
Knee	Hinge	C:	Extension	D:
E:	Ball and socket	Acetabulum and femur	F:	Gluteus maximus

(c) Identify the type of muscle fibre predominantly found in the gastrocnemius muscle of a sprinter. Identify one structural and one functional characteristic of this type of fibre. (3 marks)

Total: 14 marks

■ ■ ■

Candidates' answers to Question 1

Candidate A

(a)

Action performed	Joint	Active muscle	Type of contraction	Muscle function
Biceps curl	Elbow	Biceps brachii	Eccentric ✓	Agonist

e The candidate correctly names another type of muscular contraction, for 1 mark. However, because the phase of the action is not specified (i.e. up or down) it is not clear which muscle performs the eccentric contraction, so no further marks can be achieved. In addition, the muscle function is incorrect. Candidate A scores 1 of the 5 marks available.

Candidate B

(a)

Action performed	Joint	Active muscle	Type of contraction	Muscle function
Biceps curl ✓ (downwards phase)	Elbow ✓	Biceps brachii ✓	Eccentric ✓	Antagonist ✓

There is 1 mark available for each correct answer. The candidate has correctly given another type of contraction (eccentric) and named the phase of the action. The function of the muscle is 'antagonist'. Candidates often make the mistake of thinking that if a muscle is performing a contraction, it must be the agonist. This is a top-level answer, scoring all 5 marks.

Candidate A

(b)

Joint	Joint type	Articulating bones	Movement produced	Agonist
Ankle	Hinge ✓	Talus, tibia and fibula	Plantarflexion	Gastrocnemius ✓
Knee	Hinge	Femur, tibia and fibula	Extension	Quadriceps
Hip ✓	Ball and socket	Acetabulum and femur	Flexion	Gluteus maximus

There are a few common errors in Candidate A's answer. The fibula is not part of the knee joint. Including it in the answer renders the whole response incorrect. Quadriceps is not an acceptable answer — you must name a particular quadricep. Always check the movement produced by a muscle. The chances are that you know the correct response. Checking through your answers will clarify this. Candidate A scores 3 of the 6 marks available.

Candidate B

(b)

Joint	Joint type	Articulating bones	Movement produced	Agonist
Ankle	Hinge ✓	Talus, tibia and fibula	Plantarflexion	Gastrocnemius ✓
Knee	Hinge	Femur and tibia ✓	Extension	Rectus femoris ✓
Hip ✓	Ball and socket	Acetabulum and femur	Extension ✓	Gluteus maximus

There is 1 mark for each correct answer. This is a top-level answer, scoring all 6 marks.

Candidate A

(c) Fast-twitch fibres. These fibres have a high contraction speed ✓ and fatigue quickly.

Simply stating fast-twitch fibres is not specific enough to score a mark. There are two types of fast-twitch fibre and the candidate should have specified which type is predominantly found in the gastrocnemius muscle of a sprinter. The answer also contains two functional characteristics, rather than the one structural and one functional characteristic required by the question. Therefore, although correct, 'fatigue quickly' cannot score a mark because it is classed as irrelevant. Remember that structure is to do with the make-up of the fibre and that function relates to what it does. Candidate A scores only 1 mark.

Candidate B

(c) Fast glycolytic fibres ✓. These have a large glycogen store ✓ and fatigue quickly ✓.

e Sprinting requires maximum effort. The candidate has correctly identified the fibre type as fast glycolytic (Type IIb would have been acceptable) and has given one structural and one functional characteristic. Candidate B scores all 3 marks.

e **Overall, Candidate A scores 5 out of 14 marks; Candidate B scores 14.**

Question 2

Motion and movement

The effect of a force when applied by a performer can determine the type of motion produced. Using examples from physical education, show how you would produce linear motion and angular motion (4 marks)

Total: 4 marks

■ ■ ■

Candidates' answers to Question 2

Candidate A

Linear motion is movement in a straight line and angular movement is rotational movement. In tennis you can create topspin and backspin by hitting the ball at the side ✓.

e The candidate has explained what linear motion and angular motion are, instead of saying how they are produced. The first part of the answer is, therefore, irrelevant. There is only one example given, so another mark is lost. If the question asks for examples, make sure you give all of them. Candidate A scores only 1 of the 4 marks available.

Candidate B

Linear motion occurs when a force is applied through the centre of mass ✓, e.g. a force straight through the centre of a ball makes it move in a straight line in the direction in which the force is applied ✓. Angular motion occurs when a force is applied off-centre ✓, e.g. in a free kick, kicking the ball at the side creates spin or curve ✓.

e Here a correct explanation of how to produce each type of motion is given and there is a relevant example to accompany each answer. Candidate B scores all 4 marks.

e **Candidate A scores 1 out of 4 marks; Candidate B scores 4.**

The cardiovascular system

(a) A 17-year-old cyclist takes part in a maximal effort sprint race. Sketch a graph to show the changes in heart rate before the race, during the race and for ten minutes after the race. (4 marks)

(b) During exercise a performer's heart rate increases. Describe how neural control regulates a performers heart rate. (4 marks)

Total: 8 marks

■ ■ ■

Candidates' answers to Question 3

Candidate A

(a)

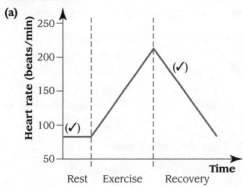

    The resting heart rate at the start is correct, for 1 mark, but the candidate does not make it clear that there is an anticipatory increase in rate. The graph then shows a sudden increase in rate, but as there is no gradual change, a mark cannot be given. In recovery, 1 mark is awarded for a quick decrease in heart rate, but as this does not become more gradual, another mark is lost. Candidate A scores 2 marks.

Candidate B

(a)

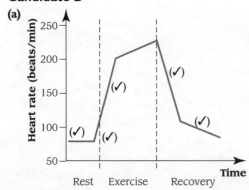

e The candidate correctly identifies resting heart rate as between 40 bpm and 80 bpm. The anticipatory rise just before starting exercise is shown. The graph shows a rapid increase in heart rate up to the accepted range of 140–180 bpm, followed by a more gradual increase between 190 bpm and 220 bpm. During recovery, there is a fast decrease in rate, followed by a more gradual decrease. Candidate B scores all 4 marks.

Candidate A

(b) Baroreceptors, chemoreceptors and proprioreceptors detect changes and send an impulse to the brain. This sends an impulse down the sympathetic system ✓ and the SA node is stimulated, causing the heart to beat faster ✓.

e This answer is correct, but because of the lack of detail only 2 of the available 4 marks can be awarded. The candidate should have described what the three types of receptor detect. For example, baroreceptors detect a rise in blood pressure. Using 'brain' is also too vague. The part of the brain (medulla) or the control centre (cardiac) must be specified.

Candidate B

(b) Baroreceptors detect a rise in blood pressure; chemoreceptors detect an increase in acidity ✓. They stimulate the cardiac control centre which controls heart rate ✓, to send an impulse via the cardiac accelerator nerve ✓. This stimulates the SA node ✓ to increase heart rate.

e This is a comprehensive, detailed answer that gains all 4 marks.

e **Overall, Candidate A scores 4 out of 8 marks; Candidate B scores 8.**

Respiration

(a) Describe the mechanism of breathing at rest and explain how this changes during exercise. **(5 marks)**

(b) Define tidal volume, inspiratory reserve volume and expiratory reserve volume. Describe the changes in these lung volumes that take place during exercise. **(5 marks)**

Total: 10 marks

■ ■ ■

Candidates' answers to Question 4

Candidate A

(a) At rest, to get air into the lungs the volume increases to lower the pressure ✓. This is done by the contraction of the intercostal muscles. When breathing out these relax ✓. This changes during exercise as more muscles are involved.

> *e* This answer requires more detail. Simply stating 'intercostal muscles' is not sufficient. The candidate should have specified which intercostal muscles are used — external for inspiration and internal for expiration. Expiration at rest is *passive*, which means the muscles relax, and it would have been better if the candidate had used this correct terminology. In this case, however, the candidate was given the benefit of the doubt. During exercise, extra muscles are used; the names of these should have been given in the answer. Candidate A scores 2 of the 5 marks available.

Candidate B

(a) At rest, the diaphragm and external intercostal muscles ✓ contract, increasing the volume of the thoracic cavity and lowering the pressure, so that air is moved into the lungs ✓. Breathing out is passive ✓. During exercise, this changes because more muscles are used. The extra inspiratory muscles are the sternocleidomastoid, scalenes and pectoralis minor ✓ and the extra expiratory muscles are internal intercostals and the rectus abdominus ✓.

> *e* There are 3 marks for describing breathing at rest and 2 marks for the changes during exercise. This is a top-level answer, scoring all 5 marks. However, candidates do not have to give all the extra muscles used during exercise. In this case, one inspiratory and one expiratory muscle used during exercise would have been sufficient.

Candidate A

(b) Tidal volume is the volume of air breathed in and out per breath. Inspiratory reserve volume is the amount of air that can be forcibly inspired after a normal breath ✓ and expiratory reserve volume is the amount of air that can be forcibly expired after a normal breath ✓. During exercise, these all increase.

e Tidal volume is not the volume of air breathed in and out. It is the volume breathed in *or* out per breath. This is a common mistake. The word 'and' changes the whole meaning of the definition. Another common error is to think that during exercise, inspiratory and expiratory reserve volumes increase. Remember these are reserve volumes. If you have to inspire and expire more air while exercising, this means there will be less in reserve! Candidate A scores 2 marks.

Candidate B

(b) Tidal volume is the volume breathed in per breath ✓. Inspiratory reserve volume is the volume of air that can be forcibly inspired after a normal breath ✓. Expiratory reserve volume is the volume of air that can be forcibly exhaled after a normal breath ✓. During exercise, tidal volume increases ✓ and inspiratory and expiratory reserve volumes decrease ✓.

e There are 3 marks available for the definitions (1 mark for each) and 2 marks for the changes that occur during exercise. Make sure you revise all these definitions thoroughly and that you know a suitable value for each, as questions sometimes require this additional information. Candidate B scores all 5 marks.

e **Overall, Candidate A scores 4 out of 10 marks; Candidate B scores 10.**

Question 5

Stages of a sprint

The diagram below shows the various stages that occur prior to, during and at the end of a sprint.

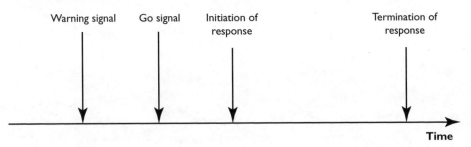

Redraw the diagram, and clearly label your drawing to identify *reaction time*, *movement time* and *response time*.

(3 marks)

Total: 3 marks

■ ■ ■

Candidates' answers to Question 5

Candidate A

Reaction time is the time it takes you to react. Movement time is the time it takes you to move. Response time is the time it takes you to respond.

> *e* This answer shows that Candidate A has not read the question carefully. It requires a *clearly labelled drawing* showing a more detailed understanding of the concepts asked. The response is irrelevant and too vague to earn any marks.

Candidate B

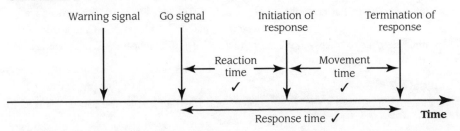

> *e* This diagram illustrates clear understanding of reaction time (from 'go' to initiation of response), movement time (from initiation to termination of response) and response time (reaction time plus movement time). This answer contains correct information that is relevant to the question set, so Candidate B scores all 3 marks.

> *e* **Candidate A fails to score; Candidate B scores all 3 marks.**

Question 6

Hicks's law

The graph below illustrates Hicks's law.

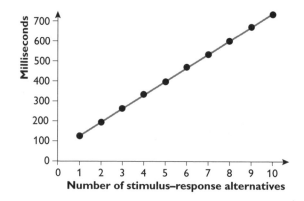

Use Hicks's law and the concept of the psychological refractory period to explain how an attacker in a team may gain an advantage over a defender. (6 marks)

Total: 6 marks

■ ■ ■

Candidates' answers to Question 6

Candidate A

I think Hicks's law states that choice reaction time is affected by the number of choices that you have ✓. If you have more choices to make, it takes you longer to react. There is a linear relationship between choices and reaction time ✓. If you double the choices, you double the reaction time.

📝 The answer about Hick's law shows good understanding. There is some repetition of points made, but generally it is a good start. The problems with this answer are that it fails to link to the practical example asked for in the question and it ignores the reference to the psychological refractory period. Candidate A scores only 2 of the 6 marks available.

Candidate B

Hicks's law states that the more choices you have available, the longer it takes to react to them ✓. This relationship is linear ✓.

The psychological refractory period (PRP) explains why it takes longer to respond to a second stimulus ✓. It can be applied in games situations when you 'dummy' an opponent (e.g. in rugby when you fake a pass but carry on running with the ball) ✓. Your opponent responds to your first signal (the fake pass), before being able to respond to the second signal ✓, which means that you can move off past your opponent with the ball ✓.

e This is an excellent response, which is relevant to the question set and scores all 6 marks. Hicks's law and the PRP are both explained and linked to a practical games example. If more marks had been available, reference could have been made to the single-channel hypothesis linked to the PRP (i.e. the need to respond to the first signal received before the second signal can be dealt with).

e **Candidate A scores 2 out of 6 marks; Candidate B scores 6.**

Feedback

(a) For a *novice* hockey player, 'effective feedback' is essential for progress.
What are the characteristics of 'effective feedback'? (3 marks)
(b) Explain how feedback differs as performers progress through the *associative*
and *autonomous* phases of learning. (4 marks)

Total: 7 marks

■ ■ ■

Candidates' answers to Question 7

Candidate A

(a) A hockey player needs lots of feedback from a coach in order to improve. This can be given while playing a game of hockey. Different methods might be used to give feedback, such as visual and verbal ✓.

    ℓ The first two sentences are irrelevant to the novice or beginner. This illustrates a common fault — the candidate has failed to answer the question set. This could be avoided by reading the question, then re-reading it and highlighting key words. The final sentence is worthy of a mark as it makes a point that is relevant to the novice performer. Candidate A scores just 1 mark.

Candidate B

(a) Effective feedback for a novice hockey player would be:
- simple and relevant to the player ✓
- clear and accurate to help the novice player focus on what is important ✓
- immediate — as soon as the action is over ✓
- relevant to the individual ✓
- provided using different methods, such as verbal and visual feedback ✓

    ℓ Candidate B scores the full 3 marks with the first three points. This is an excellent answer. It is succinct and relevant to the question set. More points are made than the marks allocated to try to ensure that the maximum mark is earned. This is good exam practice.

Candidate A

(b) As performers reach the associative phase of learning, they begin to be able to monitor their own feedback ✓. Feedback given by a coach will be a little more critical than that given at the cognitive stage ✓. At the associative stage, there will be more use of extrinsic, rather than intrinsic, feedback ✓.

    ℓ This is an excellent answer to one part of the question, with three correct, relevant points. However, there are only 2 marks available for the associative phase and 2 marks for the autonomous phase. In questions with two or more parts to them, it is essential to give a balanced answer with relevant points about each part. By ignoring the autonomous phase of learning, 2 valuable marks are lost.

Candidate B

(b) At the associative stage of learning, performers are able to monitor their own feedback ✓. It may still be extrinsic to them ✓, but becomes a little more detailed and critical to help them improve.

As the autonomous stage is reached, performers become less reliant on knowledge of results ✓ and are able to detect their own errors with intrinsic feedback ✓.

🖉 Both parts of the question are answered, with correct points made in relation to the two phases of learning. Candidate B scores all 4 marks.

🖉 **Overall, Candidate A scores 3 out of 7 marks; Candidate B scores 7.**

Classification of skills

**Performers in the women's heptathlon compete in seven different events:
100 m sprint, high jump, long jump, shot put, javelin, 800 m and 110 m hurdles.
Name, giving a *reason* for your choice, *one* heptathlon event that is mainly:**

- **an open skill** (2 marks)
- **a continuous skill** (2 marks)
- **a serial skill** (2 marks)
- **a self-paced skill** (2 marks)

Total: 8 marks

■ ■ ■

Candidates' answers to Question 8

Candidate A

- An open skill — shot put
- A continuous skill — running 800 m ✓
- A serial skill — the high jump ✓
- A self-paced skill — throwing a javelin ✓

e Questions often have words in bold print and/or italics. Particular attention should be paid to such words because they are meant to help you focus on the key requirements of the question. Candidate A's response is a basic attempt at an answer, which earns 3 marks for events correctly linked to skill classifications. However, the candidate has not justified the choice of events with reasons. This limits the number of marks that can be gained.

Candidate B

- An open skill — the 800 m ✓. The external environment may change, which requires lots of instant decisions to be made ✓.
- A continuous skill — the 100 m ✓. Running has no distinct beginning and end ✓.
- A serial skill — the high jump ✓. It can be broken down and practised in parts ✓.
- A self-paced skill — the shot put ✓. It is started when the performer is ready to throw ✓.

e All parts of the question are answered correctly. A different event is given for each part of the question, thus ensuring that no marks are lost for repetition. If 100 m hurdles had been given as an example of both a continuous skill and a serial skill, then a mark could have been lost. Candidate B scores all 8 marks.

e **Candidate A scores 3 out of 8 marks; Candidate B scores 8.**

Question 9

Theories of motor control

(a) Explain, using an example, why closed-loop theory is not applicable to all skills. (3 marks)
(b) Schmidt's schema theory is based on *four* sources of information that are used to modify motor programmes. List the four sources of information. (4 marks)
(c) How can a coach organise practices to enable a schema to develop? (3 marks)

Total: 10 marks

■ ■ ■

Candidates' answers to Question 9

Candidate A

(a) Some skills happen too quickly for feedback to be given ✓. They might be ballistic skills, ✓ which are very rapid.

> *℮* The question asks for an example. Candidate A does not give an example but the answer shows clear understanding of closed-loop theory and its lack of relevance to all skills. Without an example, a mark is lost. In some cases, examiners might be instructed not to award any marks, so where examples are asked for, give them! Candidate A is lucky to score 2 marks.

Candidate B

(a) An example of a very rapid skill to which closed-loop theory is not relevant is a high serve in badminton ✓. It is over so quickly that there is no time for feedback ✓, so no corrections can be made while performing the skill ✓. Closed-loop theory is also not applicable to novel skills ✓.

> *℮* Candidate B gives a relevant practical example at the beginning of the answer and makes three more correct points. Making more points than the mark allocation is good exam practice in trying to ensure scoring the maximum marks. In questions with relatively low marks, it is important to gain as many marks as possible, but not to waste time giving over-detailed responses. This might mean that you do not have enough time to answer properly more detailed questions with higher mark allocations. Candidate B scores all 3 marks.

Candidate A

(b) Sources of information could be a coach, a fellow performer, a teacher or the performer.

> *℮* This answer is unfortunately far too vague and all the sources given are irrelevant. This indicates that Candidate A has either not understood or not revised Schmidt's schema theory. It is important to revise all the topics covered by the specification because any one of them can be examined. Vague, general answers will not lead to success at this level. Candidate A fails to score.

Candidate B

(b) The four sources of information used to modify motor programmes according to Schmidt's schema theory are:
- knowledge of initial conditions and/or skill requirements ✓
- knowledge of response demands — what is needed ✓
- KP — knowledge of performance ✓
- KR — knowledge of results ✓

e Four correct sources of information are given, which illustrates understanding of Schmidt's schema theory. When a specific number is asked for in the question, it is important to restrict yourself to that number. If, for example, four pieces of information are asked for, examiners may be told to mark the first four responses only. Candidate B scores the maximum 4 marks.

Candidate A

(c) Coaches can help a schema develop in a number of ways. For example, they can vary practice ✓ and avoid massed practice. By varying practice, performers can develop a schema for different sports.

e This answer shows poor exam technique by focusing on one particular point, and then repeating the information. To gain more marks, the response should contain a variety of relevant facts. Candidate A scores only 1 mark.

Candidate B

(c) To help a schema develop, practices should:
- use varied practice ✓
- give feedback ✓
- be linked to the game or activity ✓
- have parts that are transferable ✓
- have lots of information ✓

e Candidate B's answer shows excellent exam technique. The number of relevant points made exceeds the mark allocation. This is to ensure that there is a possibility of earning the maximum mark. No specific number of points is asked for, so giving a short introduction to a list of bullet points is an effective way of giving a number of responses in a relatively short space of time. Candidate B scores all 3 marks.

e **Overall, Candidate A scores 3 out of 10 marks; Candidate B scores 10.**

Memory

What are the characteristics of short-term memory? (6 marks)

Total: 6 marks

■ ■ ■

Candidates' answers to Question 10

Candidate A

Short-term memory has a very limited capacity of a few items (7±2) ✓. It only lasts a short time, from a second up to a minute or so ✓. After this time, information will be lost if it is not practised ✓.

e This 6-mark question requires a much more detailed and varied response. All the points made are correct. However, a question with a relatively high mark allocation, should be given the time and exam-booklet space it deserves. Candidate A scores 3 marks.

Candidate B

Characteristics of short-term memory include the following:

- Information enters it from the short-term sensory store ✓.
- Only items receiving selective attention enter the short-term memory ✓.
- It is limited in capacity to 7±2 items ✓.
- Unless the information is put into practice, it will be lost ✓.
- Competing information interferes with information entering the short-term memory ✓.
- It is the working memory ✓.

e This is an excellent list of characteristics of short-term memory. Factual recall is all that is needed in this type of 'what' question. One or two more points could have been made to try to ensure the maximum mark. This is just in case a point made is irrelevant or repeats a point that has already gained a mark. Candidate B scores all 6 marks.

e **Candidate A scores 3 out of 6 marks; Candidate B scores 6.**

Question 11

Performance

(a) When observing the performance of a trampolinist, a coach might be trying to determine whether the performer is skilled or not. What are the characteristics of skilled performance? (3 marks)

(b) A coach 'reinforces' good performances during training by praising them. Why does this reinforcement work, rather than punishing poor performances? Explain your understanding of reinforcement and punishment in this situation. (5 marks)

(c) A swimming coach wants to improve the performance of the squad because the county championships are approaching. Using appropriate examples, what are the three main methods of guidance that the swimming coach can use to aid performance? (3 marks)

Total: 11 marks

■ ■ ■

Candidates' answers to Question 11

Candidate A

(a) A skilled trampolinist would perform in a correct way that would flow and look good ✓. The routine would be performed in a smooth manner and be aesthetically pleasing.

> *e* All the points made are correct and relevant, but they are too similar to gain more than 1 mark, which is awarded for the point made in relation to how a movement looks. To earn more marks, the candidate should have included a number of different points.

Candidate B

(a) Skilled performance is efficient ✓ with only a few mistakes ✓. It is smooth-flowing ✓ and can be adapted to situations as they arise ✓.

> *e* Four correct points are made in a succinct manner, ensuring that the maximum 3 marks are gained in a relatively short space of time. Unless the question asks for a specific number of points, it is always a good idea to try to make a few more relevant points than there are marks available.

Candidate A

(b) It is important to reinforce good performances in training by praise, such as telling the performers that they have done well. However, punishment is a negative, unpleasant experience for a sports performer ✓.

> *e* This answer is far too brief for a 5-mark question. It repeats the term 'reinforce' without rephrasing or expanding on it, which means that no marks can be awarded for this part of the answer. The candidate does attempt to answer both parts of the question, but the punishment part is far too brief. Candidate A scores only 1 mark.

Candidate B

(b) Reinforcement is something that gives satisfaction to the learner ✓ and leads to more motivation to do well ✓. Punishment is a negative experience (e.g. being shouted at and told off) ✓, which for many performers can lower their confidence ✓ and demotivate them. While reinforcement strengthens the S–R bond ✓, punishment weakens it.

✏ Both parts of this question are answered in a relevant and relatively succinct manner. It is important not just to repeat terms as they appear in the question, but to reword and expand on them in order to meet the requirements of the task(s) set. Candidate B scores all 5 marks.

Candidate A

(c) Three good methods of guidance the coach can use are visual, verbal and manual.

✏ The methods of guidance are all correct. However, they are not linked to swimming and practical examples have not been given. Therefore, Candidate A fails to score.

Candidate B

(c) The coach could use verbal guidance by using key words to help the swimmers improve (e.g. 'high elbow') ✓. Visual guidance could be used by, for example, showing videos or charts of how to do the stroke ✓. Manual guidance could be used by, for example, moving the performer's arms in an appropriate front-crawl action ✓.

✏ Candidate B gives three correct forms of guidance, along with appropriate examples, which are specifically asked for in the question. In other words, this response answers the question set — an essential requirement for exam success! Candidate B scores all 3 marks.

✏ **Overall, Candidate A scores 2 out of 11 marks; Candidate B scores 11.**